Do You Think You Are?

Understanding Your Motives and Maximizing Your Abilities

Dr Nick Isbister
and Dr Martin Robinson

HarperCollins*Publishers*

HarperCollins*Publishers*

77–85 Fulham Palace Road, London W6 8JB

First published in Great Britain in 1999 by HarperCollins*Publishers*

1 3 5 7 9 10 8 6 4 2

Martin Robinson and Nick Isbinson assert the
moral right to be identified as the authors of this work

A catalogue record for this book is
available from the British Library

ISBN 0 551 03170 0

Printed and bound in Great Britain by
Caledonian International Book Manufacturing Ltd, Glasgow

Contents

List of Figures

The following figures are reproduced by kind permission of the
publishers:

List of Exercises

Acknowledgements

The ideas in this book came out of a 'cauldron'. If there's wisdom here it's because we have had the privilege of working through them with real people in real situations. Our clients have taught us all we know. Our clients have helped us see what works and what doesn't work. Our first thanks go to them for their patience with us in our learning.

We were introduced to this way of looking at people by Art Miller Jr. Our work is based upon his pioneering work in the field of giftedness. If he didn't believe in this system as he does, then neither of us would be here today writing this book.

Both of us have benefited over the years from working with Neil Crosbie at the British and Foreign Bible Society. His ability to see the radical application of 'giftedness' for all organizations, including BFBS, has encouraged and supported us over the last decade.

Finally, the person whose insight and thinking pervades these pages most is Judy Elliman. Judy's abilities to see the implications of giftedness have both inspired us and challenged us. This book would not have been conceived or written without her constant support and encouragement.

CHAPTER 1

Where Do You Think You Are?

*Where are you
in life and where's
life for you?*

In the late 1980s a friend of ours travelled to Poland on a business trip. It was before the fall of the various communist regimes. He came back with a full repertoire of stories about things that did not work, from the heating in his hotel room to the railways on which he had travelled. The most colourful story revolved around being virtually thrown out of a restaurant simply because at 9.00 p.m. the staff had had enough and wanted to go home. Customer-focused service was not a concept that had then penetrated Eastern European society.

Being curious about people, our friend had asked more questions than most might do. He had noticed that the restaurant was vastly over-staffed for the almost non-existent trade which it attracted. Why then did they have so many waiters? One of the waiters spoke superb English and was well educated. Why then was he a waiter? His reply indicated that the communist policy of full employment meant that people were allocated to jobs on a bureaucratic basis, whether they wanted to do them or not.

The waiter in question actually wanted to be a violinist. However, 'the system' deemed that he should be a waiter and, short of a miracle, that was to be his lot in life. It was hardly surprising, then, that the service was sullen to say the least. These workers were significantly under-motivated.

How about you? Do you feel a bit like that waiter? Do you feel stuck in the wrong job? Do you feel you have been seriously misplaced in a job? Do you ever feel that, barring a miracle, you are stuck in a rut? Do you feel you've been dealt your cards and, in essence, you are never going to find a role in life that is really satisfying to you? How do you feel about your life experience to date? Do you feel that you are in the right place or do you feel that many of your hopes and dreams are substantially unfulfilled?

Constraint and freedom of choice

We might express some amazement that anyone could expect a whole population to function in such a way, yet we easily forget that the luxury of choice is a relatively recent development in the Western world. Certainly, in a medieval setting the options for most of the population were rather limited. Throughout most of human history a combination of birth and limited opportunity has actually decided the career choice of the majority of the population.

Even in an industrial society where education has been universally available for more than a century, many millions have tended to follow their parents into roles that have been 'ordained' for them – men as 'breadwinners' and women as 'homemakers'. Thus sons were expected to follow their fathers into 'good' jobs, and women weren't expected to do much more than get married, settle down and have children. The choices for women have been incredibly limited until the very recent past. The brief involvement of women in industry that was seen during the two World Wars ended as soon as the men returned from war. People were expected to be grateful to have a job – any job.

Choices for both men and women were limited and constrained by social class, so that what was a 'good' job was determined by social position. So your options, whether you went down the pit or into the family law firm, were set. Indeed, the very notion of choice was not a real category of debate; the concepts of 'duty' and the 'natural order' were more important. It was much more like the closed world of the former communist countries that our friend encountered.

Not only has freedom of choice been limited by family expectation and social convention, but even in the event that someone found a job that they really enjoyed doing, the assumption has been that the goal is always to aim for promotion, even though the very fact of promotion may significantly alter the nature of the job. The last 30 years have seen a huge change in the expectations and assumptions that critically influence the life-development that we can expect.

The new ground rules of career 'choice'

Looking at our society, it's noticeable that the old assumptions about what constitutes a 'good' career are no longer valid. For both men and women, whatever their background, the future will include each person having to make more choices, better choices and choices based on better assumptions. As we turn and face the new millennium, we must start to build for our future on the basis of some new 'ground rules'. The following five seem particularly apt now.

1 We can no longer assume that we will follow in the footsteps of our parents. Far more people than ever before are able to take advantage of educational and training

opportunities that allow a range of choices that might not have been available to previous generations.

2   We can no longer sustain an expectation that a chosen career will be a career for life. In the same way, the idea that an employer has a duty to provide lifelong employment to their employees has almost disappeared. Career changes are common between companies, between functions and between specialisms – so much so that there is little expectation that the job you begin with will be the job you end with. Retraining for a different career is part of the landscape in a world where manufacturing jobs are being replaced by service industries and where service industries are being replaced by ... well, who knows what?

3   There is a growing realization that the nature of the relationship between employers and employees has changed. When people joined an organization with an expectation that it would provide them with a job for life, the 'contract' was clear: 'You may have to put up with some things you don't like, but whatever happens you will have a job.' Globalization of business and the consequent fact that things can always be done more cheaply somewhere else, coupled with the major technological advances that have rendered so much repetitive work redundant, mean that organizations don't want to have people on their books 'for life'. This has meant that people have begun to see the relationship they have with their employer differently. People are beginning to demand that a job will provide more personal satisfaction and not merely a salary. The nature of the relationship has changed radically. As one observer of the contemporary scene, Barry Welch has noted that whereas once the organization prescribed action and behaviour, now and increasingly in the future it will seek to facilitate the individual.

Old

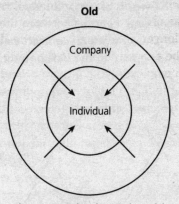

The 'command and control' model:
controlling individuals to perform to
requirements.

New

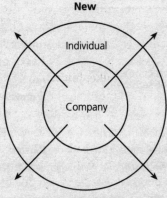

The 'new organization':
facilitating individuals, enabling
them to excel.

Figure 1i Radical change in emphasis in 'new organizations'. From Barry
Welch, *Managing to Make Organisations Work: Developing Managers for
Tomorrow's Successful Companies*, Director Books. 1992, p. 12.

Thus for the employer there are new priorities and new
aspects of managing the business that have to be given

attention. In the words of two influential commentators, there is a new 'moral' contract between the company and the individual. This new moral contract can be pictured as a 'turning upside down' of the old contract:

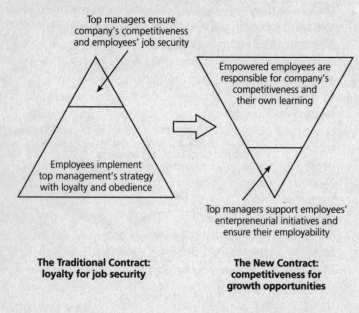

Top managers ensure company's competitiveness and employees' job security

Empowered employees are responsible for company's competitiveness and their own learning

Employees implement top management's strategy with loyalty and obedience

Top managers support employees' enterpreneurial initiatives and ensure their employability

The Traditional Contract: loyalty for job security

The New Contract: competitiveness for growth opportunities

Figure 1ii The New Moral Contract: a role-responsibility reversal. From Sumantra Ghoshal and Christopher Bartlett, *The Individualized Corporation: A Fundamentally New Approach to Management,* Heinemann, 1998.

For the individual too the nature of the contract has changed, in two ways: an immediate one and a long-term one. In the long term people want to know that they will have the training, skills, experience and 'value' that other employers may want them to have, if or when they leave their present employer. They seek long-term 'employability' – an intangible idea that usually means something like 'Other employers would give their eye-teeth to get someone with my track record'. In the short term they also seek much more personal satisfaction now. So work is measured in terms of what it does for me *now* and what it can do for me in the future. What it can do for me now is something that relates to my motivation. We want jobs that allow us to express who we are. Not only must the job provide satisfaction at a deep level, but there is no longer an expectation that the goal of every employee must be to win promotion.

4. Organizations are increasingly changing the way they work. Gone are the days when the 'boss' sat at the top of the 'pyramid' and everybody worked on the basis of being told what to do. The old 'command and control' model of organizations has died a death – death by bureaucracy. New organizations will look very different from the old, traditional hierarchies. New technology – from 'hot desking' to mobile offices to invisible networks – will make it possible for them to be so radically different. The new forms of organization that are emerging are much more like amorphous networks or 'living systems', rich in diversity and flexibility. Over the last couple of decades the traditional pyramid got turned on its head as people recognized that the 'customer' mattered. Then the inverted pyramid got 'delayered' (as new technology eliminated the need for layers of information-gatherers and interpreters) or 're-engineered' (as people recognized that some cultures or some competitors managed to do things just as well with far fewer staff). As our two influential commentators, Sumantra Ghoshal and Christopher Bartlett, have observed, organizations now look very different (see Figure 1iii).

   These organizational changes have meant that people can no longer 'hide' behind their position or the bureaucracy. Everyone's contribution and performance is more easily exposed.

5. There is a growing body of knowledge that recognizes that motivation and performance are critically connected.

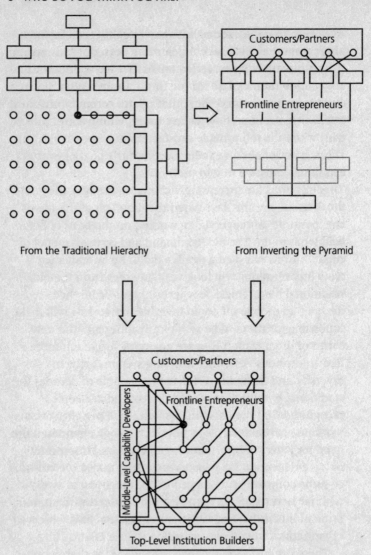

From the Traditional Hierachy

From Inverting the Pyramid

to the Individualised Corporation

Figure 1iii From Hierarchy to the Individualized Corporation. A new organization as described by Sumantra Ghoshal and Christopher Bartlett, *The Individualized Corporation: A Fundamentally New Approach to Management,* Heinemann, 1998.

Although that may seem obvious, in reality the emphasis in employment until recent years has been on skills rather than motivation. The implication is that we will tend to enjoy a job that we have the skills to do. In reality, skills and motivation are related, but they are certainly not the same. Our personal motivation is a much more complex matter than just finding a 'good skills fit'.

Nor is the issue of finding a job that works for a particular individual merely a matter of personal likes and dislikes. 'Good job fit' goes right to the heart of our identities, right to the heart of who we are and of our personal wellbeing. Experts in stress management point directly to the serious health issues that derive from poor job fit. Stress factors in employment are varied and complex. They include relationships with our peer group, our superiors and those who report to us; levels of responsibility; role conflict and role ambiguity; environmental factors such as working conditions and the length of the working day; and the pace of change in a given organization.[1]

But however important all these factors might be, one overriding consideration is the appropriateness of the job in relation to who we are. As one researcher has expressed it: 'The future will unfold at a rapid pace. Yet, there may be nothing quite as stressful as attempting to be someone different from who you really are.'[2] Indeed, Charles Handy suggests that the very future of successful organizations may rest on exploiting this notion. Really effective organizations are those that understand the value of individuals *who know themselves and who are known by their organizations:*

We live in an Age of Unreason when we can no longer assume that what worked well once will work well again, when most assumptions can legitimately be challenged. One thing, however, is clear: this is an age when individual difference will be

*important, both inside and outside organisations. The success-
ful organisation will be built around John and Peter, Mary and
Catherine, not around anonymous human resources, while in
the world outside the organisation there will be no collective
lump to hide under. We shall have to stand each behind our
own name tag.*[3]

How do you feel in your present situation? In the brave new
world of choices, of 'employability', of 'individual contribution', of 'performance' not longevity, of reward based upon
'contribution' not 'position', are you clear about who you are
so that you can make that contribution and make it well without damaging yourself? Do you really know yourself well
enough to stand behind your own name tag? Do you feel that
your present life situation reflects who you really are? If not,
then this book is for you. This book has been written to help
you answer those questions.

Making the choice

Increasingly life is about choices, but how do we make them?
For most of us, life is not a gentle, unfolding drama. It's complicated – full of uncertain choices. How can we know what we
really want from life? How can we avoid making choices that
we will later regret? Can we actively try to shape our life so
that the choices we make will bring the satisfaction we seek?

Why have you picked up this book? What is it about your
life that made you pick up the book, read the blurb on the
back and decide, 'I need this book'? You made a choice. What
prompted that choice?

Take some time now to reflect on what's going on for
you. What makes *you* want to know who you are? Before you
read any further, please take the time to complete Exercise 1.
Spend at least 10 minutes on it.

Exercise 1

Hopes for me

What are you looking for from the 'Who Do You Think You Are?' process?

What's been prompting you to think about this?

What do you hope to have at the end of working through this process?

Why *you* have picked up this book, or why *you* are seeking to explore in more depth who you are, will be distinctive to *you*. Other people have other reasons for needing to know who they are. Here are some stories of people who reached a point – often a point of crisis – where they needed to know who they were. These stories are drawn from the lives of the very many people we have worked with over the years.

For all of us, the particular stage we have reached in life carries with it very different challenges. At school it's often about possibilities. Those possibilities are often hedged with practicalities too, but there's often a sense of freedom about how things might unfold. Usually, in our twenties we are beginning to find out what we are capable of achieving. In our thirties, we have (hopefully) learned something of our potential and are working hard to establish our career. Increasingly, for many there will be the setbacks of redundancy and 'job loss'. If we weather those storms, we pick up the pieces again. Our forties begin to suggest to us that we will not achieve everything that we had earlier hoped for. In our fifties through to retirement there is often an opportunity to conduct a fine tuning of our earlier hopes. In later life we might wish to explore areas of our motivation that we missed in our early career. Each of these phases of our life offers new opportunities to utilize a deeper understanding of who we are.

Chris

When Chris finished her 'A' levels, she was uncertain what she wanted to do. All through her school life, it had simply been assumed that university would flow seamlessly on from study at a good school. She did not have a particular passion for one subject, nor did she have strong feelings about which university she should attend. Her family had been very supportive throughout her teenage years, and so, in the midst of uncertainty, the very sure advice of her parents counted for a great deal.

There was no ambivalence in her father's view: 'Get a good degree under your belt, something safe. That will set you up for a future career.' What should she do? Her best 'A' level result had been English, and so a degree in the same subject seemed the obvious choice.

Once university was over, the uncertainties of her late teens returned. The parental career advice was essentially unchanged: 'Go into something safe. After all, wasn't that what the degree was all about? Go into the financial sector – banking or insurance – or perhaps law, or even teaching.'

When none of these options seemed to appeal, her caring parents advised her to seek some professional career development help. She knocked on our door. She needed to know who she was so that she could *start* her career well. Like the traveller on the edge of the Australian Outback reading the sign that said 'Choose Your Rut Carefully – You'll be in it for the next thousand miles!', Chris started to do some reflection using the tools that you will be using in Chapter 3. She started to reflect on the activities in her life that she had really enjoyed doing.

It seems that Chris had not particularly enjoyed study. The time at university had been enjoyable enough, but the social life had taken priority over study. Her final degree results had been acceptable, but her activities outside of university life offered a more important indicator for Chris's future. Two achievements shone through her recollections and stood out for her. While still at school, Chris had developed a small business venture. The precise details of the business are not important for us to recount here. As Chris thought about the thrill she had felt in running this business, she found that the most important thing for her was the risk she had taken. The energy she had got from taking decisions that could result in significant loss to her had been a strong motivational factor.

That represented a strong contrast to the safe options commended by her parents. It provided a clue as to why both study and the suggested career options did not provide the buzz that Chris demanded.

During a university vacation Chris had taken a holiday job that had thrown up an extraordinary challenge. The catering company that she worked for had accepted a particular contract which was 'a contract too far' – they had taken on a workload that was too big for their resources. Disaster loomed, but Chris rose to the unique opportunity that presented itself. Against the odds, and without too much authority or expertise, she took over the organization of the contract and successfully managed a large team of staff (all of whom were older than her, but none of whom seemed willing to take the risk of managing the team). She pulled off a complex challenge successfully. Once again, the risk involved had produced the best in Chris. Her career choices were now beginning to take on a better definition. Whatever she did, it had to have a number of significant threads to it: it had to be 'risky', business orientated, with pressure and deadlines to meet.

Jan

Jan was in her early thirties and doing very well in her chosen career – accountancy. She was making money, both for herself and for her company, which operated in the area of corporate finance. She succeeded not just because she was technically good at accountancy but also because she liked the clients with whom she worked and they seemed to like her. On the face of it, she was well set for the future, but one small problem continually emerged.

Her employer liked the fact that Jan was making money for them and wanted her to advance through the company ranks. The difficulty for the company was that Jan seemed to be a bit of a 'maverick' in a number of areas. She was not a 'maverick' in the sense that she would do anything untoward with the numbers (though she was good at coming up with deals that were remarkable for their perception and boldness). 'Maverick' was the reputation she had gained for her behaviour in the office. She would not conform to what she saw as petty conventions. For one thing, she didn't always dress like everyone else. The signs of individuality were slight but noticeable. If others at a social event wore suits with appropriate broaches (they had all been on the 'image' course and all seemed to have swallowed it 'hook, line and sinker'), Jan would wear the suit but would annoyingly add a badge with some 'blatant' injunction such as 'Save the Whale' or 'Resist Genetic Engineering'. She couldn't be discreet; she always managed to draw attention to herself. The partners resented this. Indeed, a couple of them had even had a quiet word with her along the lines of 'If you really want to get on in this firm, you should knuckle under, play the game a bit, and not rock the boat.' One partner even suggested to her that although she might be eligible for partnership, her behaviour rendered her less suitable. Her gestures of individuality and flair were seen as acts of rebellion. Although they were slight, they were sufficient to produce a degree of unease for the company regarding her promotion to partnership.

It was time to review her future. Jan herself was increasingly uneasy. It seemed that no matter how good she was at 'doing the business', no matter how many lucrative deals she managed to conceive and broker, no matter how hard she tried to conform, she couldn't make the grade in 'their' terms. She loved her job, she didn't want to change what she did, but she wasn't sure that where she was doing it was right for her. She sought some help from us. She needed confidence in herself to face what was potentially a really big decision – should she 'hang around' for the elusive partnership offer or should she leave? The process we went through revealed that Jan did indeed desire to be unique and different. From a career point of view she wanted not just to be noticed but to be outstanding. The evidence suggested that Jan had made a good career choice, in that 'corporate finance' was a high-profile profession in which you could create a name for yourself as a 'star', but the context needed to be different. The question for the company was whether they could provide a better context for Jan. The issue for Jan was what she might do if her employer could not offer a better context for her. Being a 'grey suit' in a huge global business was just too 'grey' for her. She needed something more distinctive. She needed somewhere that not only tolerated her flair but welcomed her uniqueness and difference.

Pat

Pat had been a teacher all her life and had apparently done extremely well in her chosen career. Now aged 45, she was the head-teacher of a large comprehensive school. Advancement had come at a relatively young age with an early promotion to the position of deputy head at another school. She had been a head-teacher for some years when a devastating realization dawned upon her – she hated her job!

When she came to us and we asked her to recount past activities that she had enjoyed and done well, she was not able to think of one real personal achievement in recent years. All her fond memories of her career dated from a much earlier period in her life. There had been some exciting times. She remembered when she had taken part in an exchange programme that had taken her to Australia. She could point to some challenging field-trips and a number of overseas visits that she had successfully organized for the schools she had worked for in the past.

What was it about those past achievements that had excited her? A review revealed that she did not particularly enjoy managing people, which was primarily what her job now involved. Actually, it was not just people but a bunch of pretty demoralized people – teachers who increasingly felt undervalued by 'the system', who kept on looking to her for some inspiration. But how could she inspire them when she felt so trapped herself? But she liked teaching. She remembered the fun she used to have with classes of bright children when they really got involved in the subject she was teaching. She liked making deals, but she found there was no scope for any negotiation, as controls were increasingly imposed upon her by the local authority. She was much happier when faced with the challenge of managing difficult logistical problems. She liked to move around and to travel if necessary. She liked to produce the most efficient way of organizing people as groups rather than managing the people as individuals. If being a head-teacher were only about managing the mechanics of the organization, she might have been happy, even without the travel, but people problems always seemed to predominate. A careful period of consideration suggested that a radical career change was needed.

Gary

Gary was beginning to see retirement on the horizon but was aware that he still had some good years left in a paid working environment if that was what he chose to do. He was 56 years of age and had spent most of those years as an actuary. Gary was good at his job, but the more senior he became the less satisfying he found it. Why, then, had he become an actuary in the first place? After all, it was because he was so good at the job that he kept being promoted. Can you really not enjoy something that you are good at doing?

As he reflected on these questions, he realized that two factors had been important in his career development. First, he was technically good with numbers, and since the kind of risk assessment that he performed required good numeric skills, he had a head start. Secondly, and probably more important, he was strongly motivated by the idea of seeing fair play. He wanted to help people and felt that he could do so by ensuring, in his own way, that fair play predominated in the negotiations in which he was involved. That motivation, combined with his technical skills, gave him both the drive and the ability to do the job well. The fact that he did his job well meant that he was continually promoted. But the more he was promoted, the more he was removed from the 'coal-face' where he felt that he was actually helping people. Promotion also produced additional pressure simply to turn in good financial results – not a significant motivator for Gary.

As he turned these problems over in his mind he began to see that over the last 10 years a far greater proportion of his motivation had been coming from the volunteer work that he did outside of his job. Without realizing it, a gradual process had resulted in his job only offering something like a 30 per cent fit. He could cope with that poor fit only because his ability at the job meant that he could do it easily to the satisfaction of his employers while his real enjoyment came from elsewhere. Finally he came to feel that he wanted to do something worthwhile, and what he was doing wasn't it.

For Gary, the process of making the change to a totally different career ending was both possible and painful. He was in a sufficiently good position financially to make a change, but it was also clear that his employer was not going to make this an easy transition. He had been in the job for sufficiently long that an early exit was not convenient for his employer. A clear option was to let matters drift as they had done for many years already and simply to let the status quo predominate. He could continue to take a salary and make a contribution outside of work. For Gary the drive to make a change was significant because the job fit had become so out of kilter. He might have coped with a 60 per cent fit, but a 30 per cent fit indicated a crisis.

William

William – or Bill, as he preferred to be known – was 63 and had chosen to take retirement a few years early. He had spent the last few years as the principal of a large Further Education college and had enjoyed his career both as a lecturer and as a principal. Many of his colleagues had taken retirement a good deal earlier than he had, and he was only now taking retirement because internal changes in the college meant that this was a good time to make a change. To stay on through the changes almost implied staying on past retirement and, much as he had enjoyed the job, staying on past retirement was neither on his agenda nor on that of his wife.

The issue that Bill wanted to tackle revolved around his best use of retirement. Money was not a problem but he still wanted to be busy. But if he was going to work it would have to be something that provided all of the enjoyment that he had experienced in his earlier career, without the parts that he had not found rewarding. What clues emerged from his earlier life achievements that might help him to construct a creative retirement? What had he enjoyed in his job? A number of features recurred. He had usually looked forward to the ongoing challenge of curriculum design. That had often included negotiations with educational authorities outside of the college. Bill had enjoyed designing his office so that it had worked well for him. That design process had included some unusual demands on a desk. These were sufficiently out of the ordinary that he had actually made the desk himself.

Outside of work he had gained tremendous recent satisfaction from constructing a design for a difficult-shaped garden. He had drawn up the plans, priced the work and overseen the contractors at each complex stage of the operation. Whatever he was to do in his retirement, it would need to include a 'design' ingredient. The design element had been sufficiently satisfying in his working life that he had actually shaped his job as a series of design tasks. On reflection, he realized that it was precisely because he had intuitively perceived that the changes coming to his job would prevent him from continuing to organize it as a series of design challenges that he wanted to leave at that time.

Some personal reasons

The 'reasons' why people reach a point of crisis are legion. That's part of the point – everyone is different, and so what works for one person doesn't work for another. Chris needed risk and adventure; Jan couldn't stand the conformity expected of her; Pat got herself over-promoted; Gary needed to renegotiate the balance in his life; and Bill couldn't face years where his passion for design would atrophy in cosy retirement.

All of the people represented here faced the fact that there was a part of them that needed expression, and if that was not possible in their job, then they needed to change their context. Of course, they could have just carried on as they were. They could have recognized that they were 'unhappy' with their lot and sought to change themselves ('Be more positive'; 'Have a better attitude'; 'Come to terms with it'). They could have said, 'We'll play it safe and keep on doing what we're doing.' But that takes its toll, that gradually saps energy to the point where people say, 'Is it worth it?' Career change is about choice. It's about having courage to make changes. It's about being willing to do the work necessary to ask, 'Why isn't it working for me?' *Who Do You Think You Are?* is a guide to help you in that process. It's a way to enable you to explore the reasons why you are unhappy in your role. It is a way to help you take a long, hard look at yourself and recognize the sources of pleasure in your life and the sources of frustration. It's a process to help you address the issues you raised in the first exercise.

Maybe you have been in your job for too long. It was fun when you started it, and you found all the new learning challenging ... but now it's more like routine maintenance. Maybe you took on the role you are in now for good reasons, but those reasons have now disappeared (perhaps you were taken on to turn around the operation, and you did it – but now you are bored). Maybe you are the person who wants to do the design phase but not the implementation. Maybe it's the reverse – if someone gives you a blank sheet of paper you panic, but if they ask you to organize the *how* of turning the plan into reality, you love it. Maybe you got seduced by the prospect of promotion: you loved what you were doing in sales – meeting people, getting the deals, being on the road – but now you are the manager of those who do all that. Maybe you have just 'run out of motivational gas' because this is the umpteenth year you have been doing the same old thing. Maybe your job worked for you when you had the previous head of department, but since you got a new boss it doesn't seem the same. Maybe there's been a reorganization and you're now expected to relate to the company in a whole new way.

The reasons why you are reading this book will be as individual as you are. Now is the time to take stock and review what's going on for you.

Life stories and life stages

Maybe it's not a specific issue but more of a 'life stage' issue. Each of the stories outlined above represent a story of a life. But each of the stories also represents the story of a 'life stage'. Chris's issues were not the same as Gary's; Jan's concerns were not those of Bill.

You are at a certain stage in your life and career. We want this book to help *you* at *this* stage. Understanding the stage you are at may help you to keep the work we will do together over the next few chapters focused. 'Life stages' may be a new concept to you. Many people are familiar with the notion of a 'mid-life crisis' – that moment when seemingly secure people in their 'middle years' suddenly resign from their jobs or start affairs or buy flashy sports cars! 'Life stages' suggests that as people grow they face fairly predictable moments in their lives when major 'issues' have to be addressed – when to leave home, whom to marry, whether to have children, whether to change career, when to take retirement. When times are stable people negotiate these issues at pretty much the same times as their peers (we all seemed to get married at the same sort of time, and *now* most of us are divorced etc.). It can be helpful to think of what happens to people in organizations as having some fairly predictable phases or components. The psychologist Ed Schein did a huge study of people passing through the MBA (Master of Business Administration) programme in which he taught. From that study he concluded that as a person goes through his/her career they progress through various stages of 'developmental' concern. He represented this as a series of levels, as shown in Figure 1iv.

As you progress through your career you face a series of challenges *that change over time*. These changes, unless you anticipate them and understand them, can come as a shock and can damage your confidence – especially if you have always had only one major goal (e.g. to get myself qualified, to make it to manager, to get to 'C' grade, to make it to 'PCG' level, or however you describe the famous 'key to the executive restroom'!). The issues that you face will depend upon the 'stage' of your career.

Ed Schein's model was constructed at a time when people's career options were more predictable and stable than they are

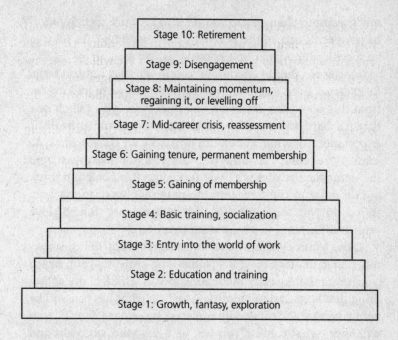

Figure 1iv Ed Schein's Major Stages of Career Issues. From Edgar Schein, *Career Anchors: Discovering Your Real Values,* Jossey-Bass/Pfeiffer, 1990.

now. Given the volatility of the relationship between individuals and organizations in today's world, it is much more likely that a person's career will go up and down this hierarchy more than once in their working life. So a person may need to retrain for a second or even third career during the course of their working life. The complexity of choices that people face now makes it all the more important to really know your gifts and motivations. The work you are going to do in this book will help you to get a secure grasp on these.

How about you? What stage of life are you at? Why is it important for you to continue to work through the process of finding out who you are? Go back to what you wrote in Exercise 1. Is there anything in what you wrote there that you might want to change? Do you need to be more specific? Or is being specific one of the problems that you have? It's hard to be specific when you don't know who you are.

Maybe we should encourage you to lift your sights a little! In Exercise 1 we asked you to say what you were looking for from this book. We created a 'contract' with you (albeit one that it's hard to quantify – you may have some unrealistic expectations of what a book can do). Now we'd like you to do some more work. This time we want you to move away from the immediate reason why you picked up this book and think a little more in the long term. Suppose we were to ask you, 'What do you see yourself doing in five years' time?' (Five years is arbitrary – you may want to try ten.)

Close your eyes now and imagine yourself doing something that matters to you – something close to your heart, something that is really motivating to you. Think about something that is central to your life – such as what job you will be doing, what role you will be undertaking, what 'identity' you will have, what context you will be using your strengths and gifts in, what activity will be filling your time. Please note *that it doesn't have to be very clear* – it can be something vague. Think of what we are asking you to do as looking up into the clouds – so everything is a bit hazy and not clearly defined. In fact, we would like you to draw what you are thinking or seeing as clouds. Figure 1v shows one person's dreams.

Now that you have seen the sort of thing we are looking for, try Exercise 2 for yourself (see p. 26). Don't worry if this exercise seems hard to you. All we want to do at this stage is to establish a point of reference for you as we delve into the 'mysteries' of who you are. *Give it a good 15 minutes of thought.*

The next few chapters allow you to explore in more depth who you are. Together we are going to try to help you to develop your own personal motivational map. That understanding represents the first stage in relating a developing self-knowledge to some key life choices.

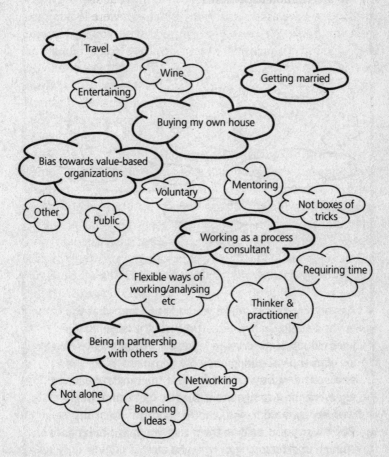

Figure 1v Sample dreams and aspirations.

Exercise 2

My dreams and aspirations

As you think about where you might be and what you might be doing in five years' time use the larger, darker-lined clouds as the ones to represent the big themes you are conscious of (running my own business, trained in a new sphere, managing a team), use the smaller clouds to represent the less significant themes (not commuting, with my own room, with another book to my credit). Don't worry about filling them all – you may not *yet* have enough understanding of who you are!

You can always change what you write here – you have choices over your life.

CHAPTER 2

Who Do You Think You Are?

The SIMA process
explained

The real-life stories in Chapter 1 may have rung a bell with you or they may not. In this chapter we are going to explain to you the basis of the 'Who Do You Think You Are?' process. This chapter will provide you with a view of the theoretical base we are building upon, a view of the model we are working with as we take you through the next few chapters.

The history of SIMA

The 'Who Do You Think You Are?' process is based upon a process called SIMA, which stands for the System for Identifying Motivated Abilities. It was created by an American called Art Miller in the 1950s. Miller was a young personnel professional working for a company in the States. One day the senior executive responsible for succession planning asked him a question: 'Do you know who the people with potential are in the organization?' Miller said that he didn't know but that he would look into how other companies identified people with potential.

So he went off and asked people in other companies. Eventually he came across an Englishman called Bernard Haldane, who had created a process called 'Success Factor Analysis' which attempted to help people find their 'enduring natural strengths'. The process involved people writing about their successes and then analysing them for repeated words. Haldane found that people's successes showed him where their 'passions' were, and the words they used to talk about them could be used to chronicle and describe those 'passions'. Miller started working with him in pursuit of his goal to identify 'potential'.

After a couple of years of working together Miller increasingly found himself disagreeing with Haldane about how to interpret the information they were getting on individuals. In particular Miller thought that he could detect deeper patterns and innate structure in the material that people were sharing. In 1961 Miller decided that he needed the time and space to develop his understanding further, so he created his own consulting business called People Management. The early work confirmed his sense that people's motivation had more shape to it than suggested by Haldane. SIMA had been created.

Since that time People Management has made the study of motivation its core competence, and the application of the system to the problems of business its *raison d'être*. We have used the technique in a huge variety of contexts. Over the last 35 years we have been working with this distinctive way of looking at people. We have worked with well over 40,000 people, male and female, young and old, from all walks of life, from all continents, from many diverse strata in society (from near-destitute prisoners and the long-term unemployed to highly successful entrepreneurs, 'high flyers' and Chief Executive Officers).

The SIMA process is still in use in a variety of high-level consulting situations. People Management International is composed of a number of specialist consulting businesses (currently there are 45 businesses on five continents licensed to use the full SIMA process in some business capacity – from executive search to out-placement to organizational development).[1] 'Who Do You Think You Are?' is the most recent application of this core 'technology' – a self-administered process built upon the SIMA process.

The phenomenon of giftedness

Over the years of working with the SIMA process, we have found that people are remarkable for the diverse ways in which they express themselves. We have found that people's passions and motivations are engaged whenever they can be in whatever context best suits them. In other words, people's motivation is irrepressible. People will find contexts in which to be themselves and to express themselves. What is not often understood is that, for those who are prepared to look, these contexts give clues as to the nature of people's gifts. 'Who Do You Think You Are?' is an introduction to that world, an introduction to the phenomenon of the irrepressible nature of motivation and giftedness.

'Giftedness' is an odd description. Most of us think of a 'gifted' person as an *unusually* talented person – a Mozart, an Einstein, a Picasso, a Stephen Hawking, a Maria Callas. Such people are indeed truly 'gifted' – they have exceptional gifts. What we are talking about is perhaps 'talent' rather than genius. Everyone has some talents, and it's these that we are going to be looking at in order to help you to see them, value them and use them better. 'Who Do You Think You Are?' has been developed to help you to identify and work with your 'talents'.

So, you may find out that you have a talent for expressing yourself on paper (you enjoy words, you enjoy the process of distilling your thoughts into clear prose, you enjoy the satisfaction of communicating through the written word) – that's your 'gift'. Others will have to judge whether the fruit of that gift is worthy of public acclaim – are you good enough to be a journalist, or to write a novel that wins the Booker Prize or a Pulitzer? That's a separate question. What concerns us here is what is the nature of a person's talent, and how can we understand and describe that talent so that you can get the best value from it and so that others will be able to benefit from it too?

We are exploring the phenomenon that others sometimes call people's natural 'competencies'. The concept of a 'competency' was introduced into the business world largely by an American writer named Boyatzis. In 1982 he wrote a book called *The Competent Manager: A Model for Effective Managers*. He defined a 'competency' as 'an underlying characteristic of a person'. Others have defined it as 'a motive, trait or skill, an aspect of one's self-image or social role, or a body of knowledge which a person uses'. Perhaps the clearest definition of a competency is: 'The set of behavioural patterns that someone needs to bring to a position, role or task in order to perform its tasks and functions with competence'.[2] Figure 2i shows how psychologist David McClelland pictures competencies.

Trainers often concentrate on the skills circle, but there are limitations to what can be done if the skill in question is not energized by an innate motivation. As someone once said: 'Never try to teach a pig to sing – it wastes your time and really annoys the pig.' When trainers work more systematically with people they often have a very mechanistic view of 'competencies'. Competencies almost become things you 'have' rather than 'are' – as if they could be singled out and worked on individually. People are much more integrated and whole than that – they are *not* just 'bundles of competencies'. If trainers work with the outer circle, counsellors and psychotherapists go deeper. They often have to work with people's self-image, or with the sources of their self-confidence.

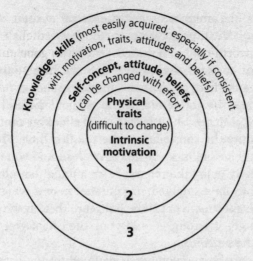

1 – How I see myself and my passion/strengths
2 – Impacted by how others see/feel about me;
how I perform in given situation
3 – What I have learnt and need to learn to build competence

Figure 2i David McClelland Competency Model. From Spencer: *Competence at Work – Models For Superior Performance,* John Wiley & Sons, 1993.

Many people have difficulty finding out what intrinsic motivation they have. The 'Who Do You Think You Are?' process has been developed to help people address this issue.

Believe it or not, we find that it is a relatively simple task. We ask people to become 'autobiographers'. We ask them to recall and then tell their 'story'. In particular we ask them to tell the story of their 'achievements'. Of course, this means that they first have to identify what an 'achievement' is to them. By 'achievements' we mean the things they have done in their life that they have (a) enjoyed doing or found satisfying, and (b) done well.

These twin criteria weed out things that have just 'happened' to them, or things that leave them feeling indifferent, or things that were unsatisfying. They focus attention on the good times, the occasions when they were at their best, the examples of their performing to the best of their ability. Although people may be naturally reticent to 'blow their own trumpet' or to 'puff themselves up', we have found that everyone, once they get past this initial hesitation, finds that they discover new and profound things about themselves.

When you first try it, it feels a bit like looking up into the sky to identify the constellations for the first time. There are just so many possibilities out there. What should you choose? Did you really enjoy that or was it something that others say you ought to have enjoyed? If you choose one achievement rather than another, what is the impact of that on the whole? Could you get it wrong? Could your choices of your stories prejudice the outcome?

Don't worry – everyone feels daunted by the prospect of finding and choosing the achievements that matter to them. Trust that the process is robust enough to accommodate these potential worries. Don't worry yet whether you can see the patterns that we say are there. The process *starts* with recollection. Analysis and identifying patterns happen in Chapters 4 and 5. For now trust that if you do the recollection, that's the best foundation you can get for the subsequent work. We can picture the process as a gradual search, as shown in Figure 2ii.

How you identify the achievements that matter to you is up to you. Some people write lists, some think of areas of their life where they have achieved, some divide their life into periods, some draw little pictures to represent what has happened to them. What you do depends a little on your motivation. The method you choose is up to you. Remember, though, that the better the quality of your recall, the better you will be set to do the analysis and pattern building required in Chapters 4 and 5. Figure 2iii (on p. 34) shows a really clear example of someone who did the recall process well.

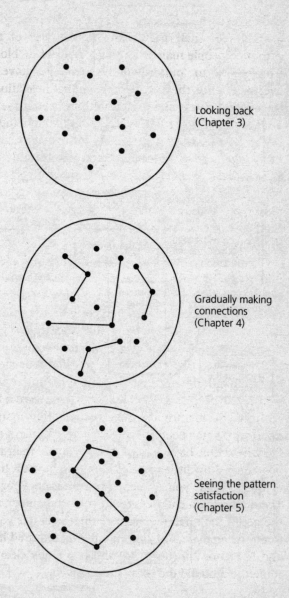

Figure 2ii Looking back, making connections, seeing the pattern of satisfaction.

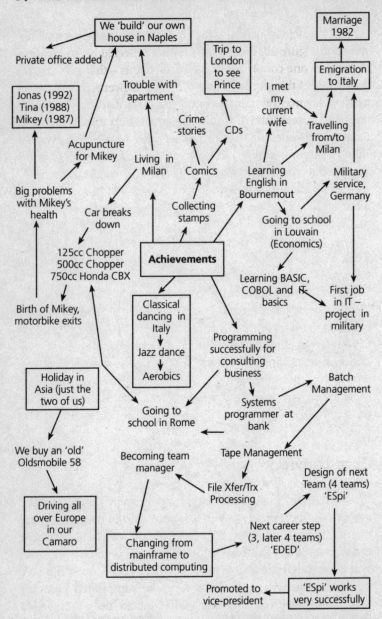

Figure 2iii Mind map of a person's achievements.

The particular person who did the set of achievements shown in Figure 2iii did it in a way that reflected his motivation (he is someone concerned to see connections – that is to say, he is a 'systems' thinker; he is also someone concerned with visual matters – hence the stamps, comics etc.). *You don't have to do anything so elaborate*. But we would like you to start something now. Exercise 3 overleaf is the *first* part of your recollection process. Take 15 minutes now to put down anything that comes to mind as an achievement to you. Try to think of as many as you can.

You've made a start … well done. Often first thoughts about what you've done are important guides to the whole process. In Chapter 3 you will be doing some more work on recalling your achievements – there's more hard work. As you start to work on it, remember that there are some real benefits to this process. The more you understand and know yourself, the better able you will be to play to your strengths; to describe your abilities to others so that they will see your potential value; to grow in self-confidence; to know how you need help if you are to function at your best. Conversely, the less you know yourself, the more prone you will be to ending up in the wrong job; the more likely you are to get 'stuck' in a rut; the more likely you are to get to a point of serious crisis. We can represent this as a set of polarities, shown in Figure 2iv (p. 37).

Core convictions

The 'Who Do You Think You Are?' process that you have embarked upon in picking up this book and in completing the first exercises is based on a number of core convictions. These convictions form the basis of how we will work with you as you go through the whole process. These convictions can be a guide for you when you have to make some fairly complex judgements later. The points which follow on pages 38–43 outline what we believe.

Exercise 3

My first thoughts on my achievements

NB: This is not a test – there are no 'right' or 'wrong' answers.

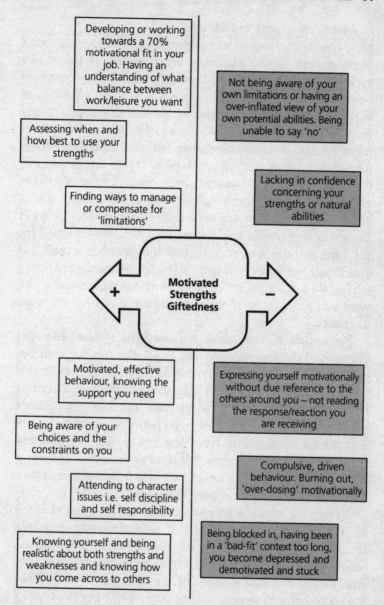

Figure 2iv Benefits of knowing yourself.

1. We are all unique individuals

Most approaches to understanding innate or intrinsic motivation or personality suggest that there are a number of personality 'types'. If we follow such an approach the closest we can ever come to understanding who we are is to say that we are most like a particular type of personality. The number of personality types varies from system to system. The Belbin Team Roles Inventory has nine, the Enneagram has nine, and Myers Briggs has sixteen. In the end *you* are going to fit into one or other of the boxes. So, like the ancient Greek myth of King Procrustes (who told people they were welcome to stay at his palace as long as they didn't mind sleeping in his bed – and when they didn't fit the bed he lopped off a few inconvenient feet, arms or legs!), *you* get fitted into the system … regardless of whether it really fits you. Hence the majority of these tests use the language of 'tends to'. But we are not interested in 'tends to'-type judgements – we want you to know with some certainty that you always work like this!

For example, one stress management system asks the question, 'Which personality are you?' The method outlines just *two* personality types – Type A and Type B. Essentially this approach suggests that the whole of the human population is either Type A or Type B. In essence, the analysis outlines extrovert personalities and introvert personalities and suggests that the two personality types respond to stress in different ways. In very general terms this is, of course, true and has a degree of value. But it doesn't take much thought to realize that life is much more complex than this.

Even if the methodology were more complex and resulted in sixteen types rather than just two, the same principle would be involved. Namely, we can either be fitted into a series of types that are like us, or we can have a description of who we are as *unique* individuals. At this level it is rather like the difference between buying an off-the-peg suit or a bespoke suit. The garment bought off the peg is as near to us as it is possible to get using a prepared pattern, but the made-to-measure, bespoke garment is made to fit us and *only* us. The 'Who Do You Think You Are?' process, based as it is on the SIMA approach, does not seek to place all personalities in one or another of a number of boxes. Instead SIMA suggests that we all have completely *individual* patterns and the approach seeks to describe every individual as a *unique* person.

2. Uniqueness is reflected in a set of unique characteristics

The unique pattern that represents who we are has a number of facets to it. Your uniqueness will be seen in the things that you love (whether you enjoy working with ideas and concepts or whether you need things that are more tangible); the 'contexts' that are conducive to you (some like risk, some can't stand it; some enjoy competitive situations, others are left cold by them; some like to know exactly what they have to do before they do it, others enjoy discovering as they go); the way you relate to others (some want to be 'contributors', some 'have to' lead); and in the 'passion' or 'drive' that underlies all these facets (some drive to 'overcome' problems, others want to 'pioneer', others want to 'control'). You have a unique set of characteristics that you need to understand *in full* in order to really understand who you are.

For example, Michael was employed by his company as a trainer. He had good communication skills, he liked working with people and had learnt enough training skills to enable him always to deliver a good result for his company. However, his core motivation was not necessarily related to communication, though that was a major ingredient in his role. Michael's primary motivation was a desire always to 'extract potential from people and situations'. His motivational drive meant that he continually sought to improve the courses he taught, to develop new courses and to find new situations in which the existing courses could be marketed. The drive to extract potential was so strong that he even saw potential where none existed! Depending on the employer, that motivational drive could either be highly valuable or something of a nuisance, but it was central to understanding who Michael actually was. Over the course of the next three chapters you will be discovering for yourself just how unique you are.

3. Your 'gifts' are a good place to start to understand who you are

Motivated abilities are related to what we can do but cannot be defined only by what we are good at. Someone might be a gifted artist, but the way in which that talent is used will be dependent on the complete motivational pattern that goes deeper than the ability to paint or draw well. In some difficult cases a person's motivation might not be obviously complemented by their ability to deliver their motivation. Derek was motivated to make an impact through public presentations. That motivation was not obviously matched by a natural ability to speak in public. He needed a context which would allow him to give presentations that included enough set visual content to enable him to make the impact that his motivation required.

4. Your uniqueness is describable

It is possible to 'map' your motivation. By understanding factors such as the context in which you thrive, the way you relate to others, your preferred learning styles, the kind of raw data you enjoy working with and the end result you desire, it is possible to construct a 'map' which will not be just a 'personality type' that you are most like but will actually uniquely describe who you are in simple, plain English. The 'Who Do You Think You Are?' process will help you to put words to your 'intrinsic motivations' and your 'competencies' and to understand how they work together as a system.

5. Your past has the 'clue' to your innate motivation

Your past experience of significant 'achievements' offers important clues concerning your motivation. As you look back on your life you can identify certain achievements which were deeply satisfying to you. Further investigation reveals that there are some common themes that emerge again and again in these achievements. These experiences represent the raw data that we can help you to use to begin to understand what motivates you. For you to get the most out of this process, it is important that you make a good start in Chapter 3 with the data.

6. Your satisfaction in all areas of your life is related to your innate motivation

How you see the world is coloured by your motivation. It affects everything you do. You view the world through the 'lens' of your motivation. You see things in all areas of your life through your innate motivation (see Figure 2v).

A deeply satisfying role will obtain an 80 per cent fit between your motivation and what you actually do with your life. Most employers work on the basis of looking for someone who will best fit the requirements of a job that already exists. Imagine for a moment an employer who starts the other way round. Suppose your current employer were to design a dream job that would exactly fit who you are. How different would your job be? It doesn't take much imagination to realize that if our job were designed to perfectly fit who we are, our levels of motivation, and so of personal satisfaction, would be significantly higher than if the fit is not good. Well-motivated employees generally achieve good results for their employer. Clearly, it would be impossible for every employer to simply invent jobs for whoever came on the company payroll. Some attention needs to be paid to the suitability of someone for the role they are being employed to fulfil. But it is rare for any employer to get the fit completely right.

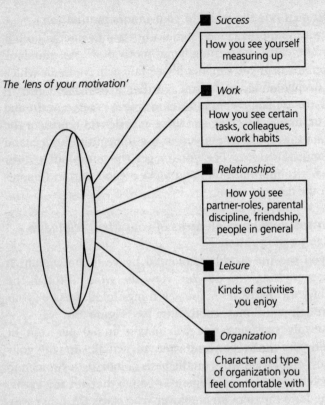

The 'lens of your motivation'

■ *Success*

How you see yourself measuring up

■ *Work*

How you see certain tasks, colleagues, work habits

■ *Relationships*

How you see partner-roles, parental discipline, friendship, people in general

■ *Leisure*

Kinds of activities you enjoy

■ *Organization*

Character and type of organization you feel comfortable with

Each of us has a unique perspective of the universe around us. We can see things that others cannot see; and in turn we can miss things that others observe clearly.

Figure 2v The profound effect of your motivation.

The better each person knows themselves and can describe themselves to others, the better the chances of maximizing the potential fit between the job and your motivation.

Good personnel development practice suggests that a job can be adjusted as time goes on either to improve the fit or to change the role or to conclude that the individual concerned needs to change jobs. This can be an unsettling process both for employer and employee, but a confident journey down such an avenue should lead to a healthier outcome for all concerned.

7. Motivation is systemic

Your motivation always works as a whole – in other words, it works as a whole system in all that you do. It does not function as a mere add-on except in very basic and limited ways. To understand ourselves we need to see how our core motivational drives work out in every part of our lives, whatever situation we find ourselves in. The pattern is always present. In this sense, motivation can be compared to a fractal picture on a computer. A fractal picture is one in which the same pattern is present no matter what part of the pattern is looked at. The overall picture is actually made up by a duplication of the same pattern at every level.

An outline of the process

It's probably time to get you started. You've had enough 'theory'. Let's get down to the process in hand. We want you to get *real*, by which we mean that we want you to

- *Review and Recall* your achievements (think back on your life to recall all the things you have done which you have enjoyed and done well).
- *Elaborate and Explore* those achievements (describe them in as much detail as you can, focusing on the 'mechanics' of how you did what you did – i.e. describe the 'activities' involved). Literally, tell *your* story.
- *Analyse and Account* for the themes present (look for the ways in which *consistency* is present; look for the pattern of behaviour evident in your achievements).
- *Listen and Learn* from the achievements (discover *for yourself* the meaning and significance of what your past

achievements tell you about what is right for you for
the future).

Telling your own story is the start of the process of being able
to say with certainty and confidence, 'This is who I am!' As a
wise man once said: 'Experience by itself simply means you
are growing older. Experience that is looked at and evaluated
provides clues that can be the wellspring of growth into your
potential.' Let's see if you can see what we are talking about in
Chapter 3.

Telling Your Story

Your chance to write about yourself!

To take your first steps in the discovery process of 'Who Do You Think You Are?' you need to do some work *now*.

You're now about to embark on the central series of exercises – finding your strengths by looking back on your life.

We'll be asking you to recall in detail things in your life which you have done well and which you have really enjoyed doing. They are your achievements. They need not be huge or dramatic, but they must be things which have given you satisfaction. They should come from different periods of your life. The work you did in Exercise 3 was the start. It was your first thoughts on your achievements. We are going to ask you to do some more reflection.

We then ask you to choose *eight* of these achievements, and consider *in detail* how you went about them. This is the 'elaborate and explain' process. As you do so, you will uncover material which is unique to you and central to you as a person. It is this data which will enable you to discover and describe your unique pattern of motivation.

So please read carefully and take all the time you need.

Review and Recall

First of all, then, you will need to spend some more time reflecting upon your life, recalling and writing down your achievements.

Remember the criteria we are using for these achievements. These must be things you have done (a) which you have enjoyed doing, which gave you some kind of real satisfaction, and (b) which you have done well. The following guidelines will help you decide what to include:

- *Your achievements must be important to YOU* – we are not interested in things which were important to your family or friends but which left you cold. We are interested in *you*.
- *Anything which gave you satisfaction is important* – no matter how trivial or insignificant it may seem. If you enjoyed it and feel that you did it well, include it. (For most people, satisfying experiences are also enjoyable. A number of people find satisfaction when they are overcoming difficulties. If you are one of those people, choose achievements which you found satisfying, even if they were painful rather than enjoyable *at the time*.)
- *Your achievements should span your life* – think of yourself as a child ... as a teenager ... as a young adult ... as well as now. Every period of your life is important!
- *They can be drawn from any aspects of your life* – if you found definite satisfaction in study ... in your work ... in leisure ... in friends and family, include it. We want to help you to build a picture from every area of your life.
- *Your achievements must be specific activities* – things you have done – not wonderful experiences, or milestones you have passed. You must be able to give concrete examples of how you worked.

As you look back on your life you will be able to see some distinct 'peaks' and 'troughs':

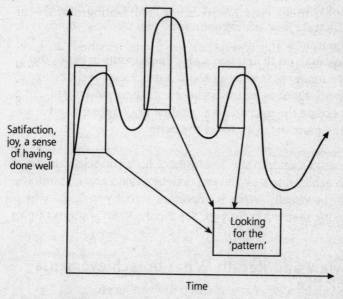

Satifaction, joy, a sense of having done well

Looking for the 'pattern'

Time

Figure 3i Searching for achievements. Scanning for 'peak' achievements illustrated visually.

Some further tips

- Don't worry if at this stage you feel daunted. Most people do, until they begin digging out those half-forgotten achievements.
- Take enough time over this exercise – it will take *several hours*, and may take several sittings. The more you put into it, the more you will benefit.
- Don't try to analyse or evaluate your experiences yet. When you remember something you enjoyed and did well, write it down. Analysis will come later in Chapters 4 and 5.

- If your activities took place with one or more other people, describe what *you* did. If you did nothing differently from others, describe what all of you did.
- Don't be modest! You are the key actor in each event. They are *your* achievements and you can be completely honest.
- We ask you to describe *eight* achievements in detail, but you may want to write about more. Please feel free to write about as many as you want. These stories will become the data you will analyse in Chapters 4 and 5, so the more data you have, the better.

It doesn't matter in the first instance how you select and recall your achievements – you can do it by subject areas, chronologically or visually. What is important is that you find a way of working that works for you. See Figure 3ii for some examples.

Review and Recall: What do achievements look like?

If you are not sure what 'achievements' might look like, here are some examples. These are taken from lots of different people. Your own selection or list isn't likely to be so diverse! Don't worry if some of the achievements seem different from yours. That's the whole point: you *are* different.

Childhood
- Became a tree-climbing champion, beat all the boys in the village, even though I was a girl and really small for my age.
- Developed my own technique for multiplying large numbers. I always managed to do well in maths tests.
- Gave my first solo at a school concert, playing the cornet.

Sport   first team
             high jump
             sprinting

Work   designing brochures
             organizing dept
             training new assistants
             changing attitudes
             building up a team

Home   3 grown-up children
             good relationships
             coping with John's illness
             new life after divorce
             gardening – built pond

Prize for reading, age 9
Book review, age 12
Paper round, age 14 to 16
Ran car boot sale
successful event, 20s
Did up old furniture and resold it,
started a business, 30s
Articles published, 40s
Golf competitions, 50s

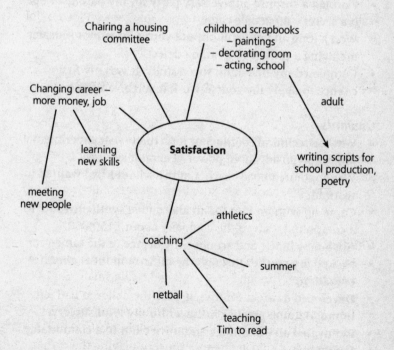

Chairing a housing
committee

childhood scrapbooks
– paintings
– decorating room
– acting, school

Changing career –
more money, job

adult

learning
new skills

Satisfaction

writing scripts for
school production,
poetry

meeting
new people

athletics

coaching

summer

netball

teaching
Tim to read

Figure 3ii Overview of different ways of finding your achievements.

- Took on my first acting role – played Noah at primary school – and overcame my childhood stammer.

Teens
- Started a school rock band – I played the organ and worked out most of the music and arrangements.
- Selected to play for my school hockey team.
- Rescued a cat and found its owner.

Twenties
- Produced an original photograph which was chosen by the local newspaper for an award.
- Passed my driving test first time.
- Planned a surprise anniversary party for my parents. Kept it a secret – 40 people came.
- Won a long and difficult dispute with a large motor dealer involving a car with a gearbox defect.
- Completed my first audit successfully. It was my first chance to apply my course-work to a real situation.

Onwards
- Was the technical coordinator for a three-year experimental project on an advanced power-generator system.
- Was appointed head-teacher at the school I had wanted to work in.
- Came up with an idea for an alternative synthetic route to a compound – saved the company about £150,000.
- Got a new house and acquired my degree in the same year.
- Nursed my mother through the difficult months after her operation.
- Developed a career for myself once the children had left home. Became practice manager for my local surgery.
- Renovated an old cottage and turned it into a comfortable family home.
- Took up skiing and eventually became an instructor.

Elaborate and Explain: Exploring what those achievements were

The final step for you is to describe in detail *how* you went about doing your eight selected achievements. Here are two examples from two different people:

Becoming a Pogo champion

'I mastered the Pogo stick to the stage where I could Pogo anywhere – no hands! The Pogo stick was a gift. I have two brothers with whom I played in our back garden. The garden was slightly raised, and at the house end there was a yard. My brothers and I took turns to see how many jumps we could do on the Pogo stick. They soon got bored with it and settled with a few jumps. I kept going, despite many scraped shins and bruised elbows – I was determined to master the beast. Left on my own, I discovered that the hardest part was getting started, and that was knocking my confidence. So I worked out that by standing on the raised part of the garden I could get onto the pegs much easier. From there, I worked out that the next problem was the stick hitting the ground at an angle, so I worked on a technique for holding it with my knees so that my hands were free. From there it was just a matter of practice. I just kept at it. As I got better and better, my brothers started taking more interest, and so did my parents. I don't seem to remember anyone else having one, so it was pretty unique. As others saw what I was doing they seemed interested, so I started helping them. I used the same technique that had worked for me. I enjoyed the experimentation of finding out what worked and then sharing it with others. I felt good because I had showed more determination than my brothers. I also found an approach to solving a problem that was quite innovative and yet systematic and, most importantly, it worked.'

Taking Sophie out for walks (aged 14)

'I used to take Sue's 18-month-old baby out for a walk, which gave Sue a break to get on with cooking the tea or something else that she needed to do that day. When I knocked on the door after school once or twice a week, Sue was always really pleased to put Sophie in the buggy and send her off for a walk or a trip to the park. I tried to be very careful. I did not take the buggy across any main roads or leave it outside any shops. If she started crying a lot or if it began to rain or got very cold, I would take the baby home to her mum.

'I would often take Sophie to the park and give her a go in the baby swing. If it was a particularly sunny day I would take a blanket with me, place it in the shade under a tree and sit and read to Sophie. I would bring her favourite books and some apple juice and biscuits. We would then return home. I was always careful to arrive back home by the time Sue told me to.

'It was satisfying to be considered responsible and grown up, to be trusted. I liked giving Sue a break and taking a real baby out.'

Remember: Each person has achievements that are significant to them. Your achievements will be different from the ones we have just shown you!

This is not a test. There is no time limit and there are *no* right or wrong answers. Thinking about your life in this way will provide important data about you and your unique motivational pattern. It is *your* data, written about *your* experiences, in *your* way.

You will not be able to do anything else with this book until you have done this exercise for yourself.

However you like to work, it is now your chance to tell *your* story for *yourself*!

Exercise 4

Telling my story

Please use this part of the book in the way that suits you best. You may want to photocopy the following pages or make pages on your computer, using this format as a guide. If you are using a PC, don't spend time creating pages in our graphic format; just type your achievements.

If you are writing by hand, please use black ink, as you will need to do some significant work on the text later.

This is a working document and we are going to ask you to do some analysis on it in Chapters 4 and 5, so make sure that you have left space for your analysis.

Before you begin, please make sure that you have read the first part of this chapter, which explains what we mean by 'achievements' and how to go about reviewing your life. It also provides examples to follow. Only when you have read *these guidelines* will you be in a position to begin.

This is an important phase of the 'Who Do You Think You Are?' process. Please give yourself the time and space you need to do justice to it (the whole recall process can take anything up to four hours).

Elaborate and Explain

Go back to the preliminary list of achievements that you
made in Exercise 3. Now try to list your achievements in
approximate date order, using the headings below as a
guide.

Childhood

Teens

Twenties

Thirties

Forties

Onwards

(If you haven't reached an age indicated here, cross out the irrelevant age and use the space to add more examples.)

Other achievements (ongoing or sustained over a period of time)

Selecting the key achievements

When you have decided that you have done enough recollection, you need to select *eight* achievements to expand on. It is important to choose them from *different* periods of your life, and to include at least one from your childhood or early teenage years.

Exercise 5

Selecting eight key achievements

Look at your list of achievements and choose *eight* that are particularly important to you. Choose examples from your whole life if possible, and don't worry about the order of importance. Give each achievement a short title and list them below.

1.

2.

3.

4.

5.

6.

7.

8.

Focus

Having chosen your eight achievements, describe in detail how you went about doing each of them, using the forms on the following pages. One form is provided for each achievement. It may help to refer back to the example of the 'Pogo' stick champion earlier in this chapter. This is the final step of the elaboration phase, and it forms the basis of the analysis and accounting process in Chapters 4 and 5. As you think and write, you may begin to see themes already emerging.

Exercise 6

My eight achievements

Achievement 1
What was the achievement?

How did I get involved?

What did I do?

What did I find satisfying about it?

Achievement 2
What was the achievement?

How did I get involved?

What did I do?

What did I find satisfying about it?

Achievement 3

What was the achievement?

How did I get involved?

What did I do?

What did I find satisfying about it?

Achievement 4
What was the achievement?

How did I get involved?

What did I do?

What did I find satisfying about it?

Achievement 5
What was the achievement?

How did I get involved?

What did I do?

What did I find satisfying about it?

Achievement 6

What was the achievement?

How did I get involved?

What did I do?

What did I find satisfying about it?

Achievement 7

What was the achievement?

How did I get involved?

What did I do?

What did I find satisfying about it?

Achievement 8

What was the achievement?

How did I get involved?

What did I do?

What did I find satisfying about it?

CHAPTER 4

Starting to Find Out Who You Are

Making sense of your story

If you have done the work in Chapter 3 you have 'told your story'. You will also have collected some significant personal data. Well done! We are now ready to move on from the 'elaborate and explain' phase (given our desire to help you get *real*!). Chapters 4 and 5 will be concerned with the next phase – 'Analyse and account' – but first we need to set a couple more things in train.

The first thing we want you to do with this data is to *let it tell you what you need to know*. As you were going through the 'review and recall' and the 'elaborate and explain' phases of the process, what were you conscious of? What were you aware of? Did the things you identified tell you anything about yourself? Where are your achievements from? What period of your life do they cluster in? Can you see any immediate connections or patterns? We are jumping the gun a bit here because this is really 'listen and learn', but it is important to consolidate what's going on for you. *We don't want to impose an interpretation of your life on you.* We want *you* to learn how to

read what you have done, how to let it tell you what it can. So
please complete the following exercise *now*. Give it 10 minutes.

Exercise 7

The themes I have seen already

We are going to build on that understanding now, but first we need to explain the structure of your motivation in a little more depth.

We believe that the way you are motivated to work has 'structure' or, more accurately, that it's *systemic* – that is to say, how you function is as a *unified whole*. Your motivation has 'shape' to it. Before we can help you to see the *particular* shape that *your* motivation has, we need you to get an overview of motivation in general.

We have been working with people's 'stories' for over 35 years. During that time we have analysed well over 40,000 'stories', looking for the structure and pattern in each one. These are the stories of people describing things they have done which they have enjoyed and done well. *Your* story is the latest one of these. From all of that rich variety, from all of the different countries we have worked in, from the incredible diversity of contexts and particular experiences that people have shared with us, we have found that it is possible to see a 'structure' in each person's story – to see a 'pattern' in each person's achievements.

We want you to see the 'consistencies' in your behaviour. We want you to see a 'system' in the way that you work. We can picture this in the way shown in Figure 4i.

Behind each of your achievements there is a structure of motivation. The 'Who Do You Think You Are?' process is an attempt to describe your strengths as a whole. The picture painted of your strengths is based upon an extensive process of review, reflection and analysis. The conclusions we want you to draw are a synthesis of the *consistent* themes in *your* life. Your strengths work together predictably so that over time it is possible to observe a pattern in your behaviour. Your pattern is unique. You are motivated in ways that are *distinctive to you*. Your strengths are not mere random, haphazard collections of things you may or may not use. You are a complex system with abilities that work in harmony

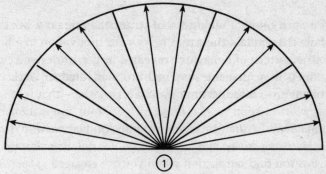

Describing your first achievement, you focus upon particular aspects of 'reality';
you only remember certain things. We can represent each of these by arrows.

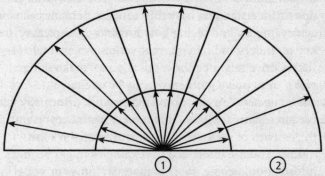

The next achievement you choose again has certain aspects that you recall.
Whilst not all things follow through, some do.

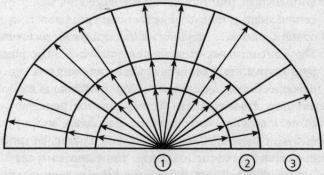

As you add your achievements again you keep on
focusing on certain aspects that matter to you.

Figure 4i Representing the task of describing your achievements.

with each other. The pattern of your behaviour is a working whole that has a structure.

The pattern of behaviour revealed in the stories you have outlined in your achievement history in Chapter 3 can be broken down into five important facets:

1 *Motivational drive*. In all your motivation you have an *underlying driving purpose*, a 'reason' for doing all that you do. You find satisfaction when you are engaged in specific processes or complete a certain specific outcome or achieve certain kinds of results. We call this your motivational drive. Understanding how this 'essence' pervades all your achievements, and seeing how it works dynamically, is a key to understanding your motivation. An example of such a drive might be the motivation to 'make things work' or to 'solve problems' or to 'be in charge'.

2 *Subject matter*. You are motivated to work principally with certain *selective* subjects. This subject matter represents the essence of *what* you like to work with – it's the 'things' you are interested in. Examples might be ideas, information, people, money, material things or visual subject matter.

3 *Circumstances*. Your motivation is engaged not simply by certain subjects that you like working with but also by *certain conditions or particular contexts or a specific environment*. These circumstances describe the *situational* components of your motivation. Examples might be working to a deadline, having a clear goal, using something as a jumping-off place, where there is 'potential', a team context, or where there is a chance to save money.

4 *Motivated abilities*. When working with a particular subject in a certain set of circumstances, you consistently use certain *abilities*. These abilities are different from mere capabilities that you might also have. There are many things you 'can' do, but what we are describing is what

comes most naturally to you or what you consciously enjoy doing. These abilities describe what you *love to do*. They are the ones that you engage whenever you have the opportunity. You do not tire of using them. These abilities describe the *how* of your motivation. These strengths we call your *motivated abilities*. Examples include organizing, planning, building, influencing, designing, leading, communicating and so on.

5   *Relationship*. Within your motivation there is an interest or concern to move into a particular relationship with others. This aspect of your motivation explains how you work best with other people, or what role with other people suits you most – it's a way of describing how you like to be with others. Examples might include being a 'spearhead', or part of a team, or a liaison, or a representative, or a catalyst, or being in a defined role.

So there is a *pattern* in your behaviour. In SIMA we call this your *Motivated Abilities Pattern* (MAP). All five aspects of motivation fit together as a systemic whole. Here we are just going to call it your motivational pattern.

Thus your motivation, as revealed in the stories you have recounted in the previous chapter, has all these five components. They are a 'system' – they all work together *dynamically*. There is a 'flow' involved in how you work. We can represent that diagrammatically. Your motivation can be 'tracked' over time, as shown in Figure 4ii overleaf.

This picture of a person's motivation as a process of 'flow' is an adaptation of a model of personal activity called the 'Gestalt cycle of experience'. We came across the picture in a series of articles on Gestalt psychology. The Gestalt cycle of experience is a way of representing how people function and is drawn from a school of psychotherapy that derives from the work of Fritz Perls. The German word *Gestalt* means 'whole', and Gestalt psychology is a way of looking at people as

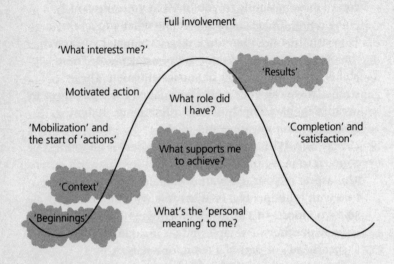

Full involvement

'What interests me?'

'Results'

Motivated action

What role did
I have?

'Mobilization' and
the start of 'actions'

'Completion' and
'satisfaction'

What supports me
to achieve?

'Context'

'Beginnings'

What's the 'personal
meaning' to me?

Figure 4ii Overview of the 'flow' of an individual's motivation.

'whole', 'self-organizing', 'self-integrating' individuals. It's a
way of looking at people that is very congruent with all that
we have learnt about people over the years through the SIMA
Process. The Gestalt cycle of experience attempts to represent
the 'purposefulness' and the 'sense' of people 'in process'. As
one commentator has observed:

> *It involves not only* sensations *and* perceptions, *but also con-
> cepts of a complex character,* feelings *and* desires *in respect of
> the end desired, and* volitions *in respect of the act intended;
> and all of these elements are fused and blended into one unique
> purpose; which is then put into* action *or* execution.[1]

Gestalt psychology helps people to become aware of what is
happening to them in the 'here and now'. We have adapted
the basic idea and linked it to aspects of personal motivation.[2]

Although we are using the concept of 'flow' as described in Gestalt psychotherapy, we could equally have linked this state of 'being in the flow' to that which Daniel Goleman has described in his book *Emotional Intelligence*. 'Knowing yourself', 'being aware' of yourself in as much depth as you can, being conscious of your feelings and your thoughts as you engage in action, is at the heart of 'emotional intelligence'. The work we are going to do in the next few chapters should help you to become aware of yourself 'in the flow'. Paying attention to the dynamics of your motivation can be very liberating.

The task in this chapter and the next is to help you to see this 'flow' and all the individual components for yourself. In order to do that we need to help you to start to make some sense of these categories in relation to your *own* achievements. We need to help you to make some distinctions.

Find some coloured highlighters (you are going to need five different colours). Each colour will represent one of these five broad categories: your underlying drive; the subject matter that interests you; the particular circumstances that are motivational to you; the abilities that you love to use; and the way you seem to operate with others. At the top of the pages you have written make a note of the colour code you will be using.

The rest of this chapter and the next chapter will be about helping you to 'analyse and account for' your achievements using these categories. We are going to help you to go back through your stories and treat them as achievement 'data'. Those data will be the building-blocks upon which we will then help you to paint a portrait of your strengths. This is a 'tracking' process. We are going to ask you to go back through your stories to 'track' what happened, to find and describe what you did, to make yourself aware of what is significant and important *to you*. You may know some things already – that's good. You may have become aware of more things as you wrote – that's good too. The chances are, however, that you don't know all you *could* know about yourself from the stories you have chosen. You need to do some more detailed work.

Given that what is needed next is some protracted, detailed analysis, this may not be your forte. The activity of analysis, or the subject matter you are working with – words – may leave you cold. As you come to contemplate the task, you have to be aware that your motivation itself will come into play – that is to say, since what we are asking you to do is to become your own researcher/analyst, this may not fit well with your motivation. We are going to ask you to act like an 'accountant', patiently tracking the evidence you have provided to come to a fair, sound view. You may *not* be a person motivated by such detailed work. You may *not* enjoy reading stories (even your own stories) with a fine-toothed comb. You may *not* enjoy sitting at a desk by yourself analysing words. That's OK – not everyone does. However, we still need to find a way to let *your* story speak to *you* – to let your story show you where your motivation finds its best expression. As we see it, you have *three* choices:

1 *Put your head down and 'slog' through it!* If the prospect of doing this activity makes your heart sag, makes you wonder whether there is anything on the TV, makes you feel flat – that's data too. Listen to what that's telling you about the things that interest you. You have got some choices here. Think of the things that have helped you get through activities you haven't liked in the past (e.g. if you do this exercise you will reward yourself with a walk with the dog, or a coffee and a biscuit, or a visit to the gym – whatever will work for you, try it). This work of analysis only suits *some* people, so find a way in which it can work *for you*.
2 *Find someone you trust who has the motivations you need!* Do you know someone, *someone you trust*, who would be willing to help you? Such a person would need to have

some specific strengths – namely, being a researcher/ analyst – someone whose behaviour indicates to you that they love analysing data, categorizing words, interpreting information. Can you think of anyone you know who loves solving complex puzzles, doing crosswords, tracking down data? Could you 'cut a deal' with them – you will do something you like doing *for them* if they will read this chapter (to familiarize themselves with the task and to get the categories clear) and do the analysis of your story *for you*. If you choose well, you may even find that you have won a good ally as you begin to act on this to make changes to your life.

3 *Give the first part of it a go and see how it is for you. Then consider whether or not you need to adopt an alternative strategy!* If you are not sure yet whether this part of the process is good fun for you, the best thing to do is to give it a try and see how you get on. The easiest way to see whether or not this is going to work for you is probably to 'track' something in your own achievements. There are *ten* steps to the process of analysis (six steps are outlined in this chapter and four in the next). We suggest that you try the *first* step now, then review whether you want to do the rest after that. If you try it and it is really tedious for you, then you may need to revise your strategy.

Using the picture of the flow of your motivation (see Figure 4ii) as a guide, we can break down the process of analysis and accounting to ten key steps. These can be represented on the 'flow' diagram as shown in Figure 4iii.

The task of 'analysis and accounting' thus has ten steps. These are:

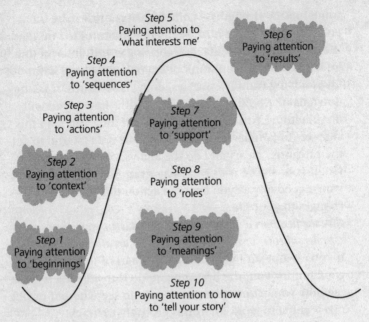

Figure 4iii Overview of the steps of analysis and accounting.

Step 1	Paying attention to 'beginnings'
Step 2	Paying attention to 'context'
Step 3	Paying attention to 'actions'
Step 4	Paying attention to 'sequences'
Step 5	Paying attention to 'what interests me'
Step 6	Paying attention to 'results'
Step 7	Paying attention to 'support'
Step 8	Paying attention to 'roles'
Step 9	Paying attention to 'meanings'
Step 10	Paying attention to how to tell your story!

As you go through these steps you are going to record the information you find in a working document. If you turn to page 165 you will find a section called 'This Is Me At My Best'. That is the correct place in which to record your analysis.

Have a look at what you wrote in Exercise 7, 'The themes I have seen already'. Where do those themes 'fit' in this series of steps? As you work through the steps carefully, feel free to add the themes that you've observed already at the most appropriate point.

Step 1: Paying attention to 'beginnings'

Step 1 is all about 'beginnings'. We are going to start the process of analysis with *how you got started* in your achievements. Here are some typical things that people say about 'beginnings':

- 'I was invited to take on the role.'
- 'To have someone say to me that I could not do it was tantamount to a challenge.'
- 'When I knew that there was a competition involved, well – you couldn't hold me back!'
- 'Since I had never done something like this I was keen to give it a go!'
- 'Naturally, I didn't push myself forward, but when the team unanimously voted for me, what could I do?'
- 'My parents didn't know what I was doing, so it was a great opportunity.'
- 'Of course, when I saw that my friend wasn't as interested in the round as I was, I suggested to him that he should let me take on his round as well as my own. He was well pleased, and so was I.'
- 'In the place where I was staying there was a group of us, so naturally we tended to do things together, so when someone said "Let's have a Christmas party," all of us fell into line.'
- 'I suppose my collection started when I inherited my grandmother's set. I just went on from there.'

- 'When my father was killed, naturally I had to take on responsibility for looking after the farm.'
- 'My love of cooking comes from my mum. I used to watch her in the kitchen, and I guess I just picked it up from there.'
- 'Some say I was landed in it, but I don't see it like that. When my boss had the heart attack the day before the presentation, what else could I do? I didn't sleep at all that night, but I managed to get everything set up.'

How about you? *How* do your achievements start? What's the *specific* trigger to you being motivated? 'Beginnings' are important components of the 'circumstances' that motivate a person. Take the highlighter that you have selected to represent the 'circumstances' and read through your achievements, paying particular attention to the 'beginnings'. Go back over what you have written and look for the beginnings for you.

Looking at your 'beginnings', are there any common threads that you can see? Although your achievements may all be very different, is there something that seems significant in how they all started for you? When you have highlighted anything that looks significant to you (the statements you have highlighted describe *how you got involved in or started on* something) compare what is highlighted with the following categories of trigger.

Do they include you …

- responding to needs?
- enjoying something that is new or different to you?
- starting with problems?
- pursuing causes?
- taking up challenges?
- meeting tests head-on?
- being engaged by competition in head-to-head situations?
- striving in competition against some standard or record?

Perhaps …

- emergencies get you fired on all five cylinders.
- you are someone for whom overcoming some disadvantage or handicap is part of how you are 'wired'.
- it was the mere fact of being asked or invited that started the whole thing for you.
- you are someone who sees everything as an opportunity or an opening.

This is *not* an exhaustive list. What other aspects of your beginnings seem important?

Your achievements as told in your story have the answer. To 'track' your achievements, looking for the *specific* circumstances that triggered you, is to respect your own individual process. To note what gets you started is to begin the task of tracking your motivation. 'Beginnings' are very important. If we were to ask you to complete a complicated construction activity, you would be lost from the beginning if you didn't pay attention to how the process *starts*, if you didn't get the foundations right. So as you come to build upon your history to construct new and better 'futures', pay attention to 'beginnings' and pay attention to how your achievements started.

What have you found? In the section headed 'This Is Me At My Best' (p. 165) the first question says: 'What do I think gets me started?' In the box marked 'evidence' write down the words or phrases you have highlighted as 'beginnings'. When you have a full set in the box, look at them and see if they have any common themes. In the space marked 'What do I think gets me started?' write the words or categories that seem common. On page 172 you will find a form that has been completed as an example. This should help you to see what the finished product looks like. Don't worry if you are not sure. Write the words in pencil if you want to be able to change them later. *You* are going to be the ultimate judge of how true the finished portrait is, so if you are not sure of something, just put it down tentatively. The evidence box should help.

When you have completed this task, *stop and check* to see whether this is something you enjoy doing and find easy. If it is, then you can press on. If you have found it hard to track and analyse, perhaps you need some help from someone you trust. Maybe you don't need someone to do it all for you, but you do need someone to discuss it with. Pay attention to what you need to help you – this is significant data (it might indicate something that is important as 'support' to you). Whatever you decide is OK, provided that you find some way of engaging in this process of analysing and tracking, because the rest of this chapter and the next is nothing but that!

Step 2: Paying attention to 'context'

To be clear how you got started on something is a start. Well done! But it is only that. We need to be clear what *other* circumstances help to *keep* you interested and motivated. Remember, the 'circumstances' of your achievements characterize the 'context' that is good for you. Take your highlighter again (the same colour) and mark anything that seems significant to you in the way that you have described your achievements which relate to the context of the achievement ('We were in a team'; 'I had been given clear instructions'; 'I had a clear deadline'; 'There was considerable pressure to deliver'; 'The goal was obvious'; 'I had the time I needed to do a quality job' etc.).

When you have highlighted anything that looks significant to you (the statements you have highlighted describe what *kept you interested* in something) compare what is highlighted with the following categories of sustaining circumstances:

- Do you like circumstances that are unstructured and fluid situations?

- Are you someone who likes structured, ordered situations – perhaps even routine, scripted situations?
- Do you like clear responsibilities and defined objectives or roles?
- Do you need instructions and specifications to be available to you?
- Do you like contexts where there is growth and the potential for development?
- Do you see things that others don't; do you see the potential in people or things; do you see the possible rather than the known or the sure?
- Do pressure and positive stress motivate you?
- Does lack of pressure make all the difference to you?
- Do you need deadlines and constraints?
- Do you find it motivating to be exposed to risks or hazards?
- Do you find that you are not really engaged until you have some difficulties or obstacles to overcome?
- Do you like immediate response?
- Do you need learning time to be available?
- Do you enjoy the chance to travel or move around?
- Do you enjoy the chance to get outdoors or to be in a natural setting?

This is *not* an exhaustive list. What other aspects of your context seem important?

What have you found this time? Again, turn to 'This Is Me At My Best' (p. 166). The second question says: 'What do I think keeps me going?' Under that question write down any words that you think make sense of the things you have just highlighted. Again, don't worry if you are not sure. *You* are the judge of how true the finished portrait is.

Step 3: Paying attention to 'actions'

So far we have concentrated on the 'circumstances' – we have looked at what *starts* you and what *sustains* you. But by now, in any achievement you are pretty much engaged. To be 'engaged' is to be *doing* something. What did you do? Take the highlighter that you have designated for the 'motivated abilities' (it should clearly be a different colour to the one you have been using so far!). Motivated abilities are actions or activities that you enjoy doing. The clues to these abilities in your achievements are the verbs you have used ('I *designed* the picture'; 'I *read* the book with intense interest'; 'We set about *organizing* it'; 'We really *planned* it well'; 'I *built* the shelf'; 'I *ran* as hard as I could'; 'I *coordinated* the programme'; 'I *pictured* what I wanted' etc.). Go back through your achievements and highlight any verbs you used.

What have you found now? Again, turn to 'This Is Me At My Best' (p. 166). The third question says: 'What do I do when I am motivated?' Write in all the verbs you have just highlighted. List them *each* time they occur (that may be significant), and list them in their various forms (you may have used synonyms for the same activity). Make sure that you get all the examples of your 'doing' something (by 'doing' something we mean any activity that contributed to the achievement, including things that were clearly not 'doing' anything, like 'thinking', 'learning', 'planning', 'dreaming' etc.). Again, don't worry if you are not sure. *You* are the judge of how true the finished portrait is.

Sometimes, when people get to this point they seem to discount the value of what they are seeing. They say about themselves, 'Well, that's no great shakes! Doesn't everyone plan? Doesn't everyone learn? Doesn't everyone organize?' It is natural for you to feel as if what you are describing is OK but nothing special. Indeed, sometimes these very abilities are ones that others have disparaged or put down ('She's such a day-dreamer'; 'Oh, you're so fastidious! Why do you have to get it right?'; 'Look, can't you just lighten up? Why do you have to plan everything so carefully?'; 'Now we'll have to wait while he considers all his options'). How often have people said to us, 'Who do you think you are?' To have an opinion? To think of yourself as important? To think your strengths are any good? The 'Who Do You Think You Are?' process is a way for you to find and affirm your strengths. As you track back in your achievements and see examples of yourself organizing, preparing, influencing and doing, you are beginning to find the 'gifts' you have got. Let us say here that we have the beginnings of your 'competencies'. These are special because they represent the very best you have to offer any potential employer. They are the things which potentially can differentiate you from others, which make you stand out from the pack. They are the basis on which you can build a successful career. They are the real 'value-added' *you* that you bring to any role.

Having listed these verbs, you will need to 'unpack' some of them a little. Let's take the word 'plan'. Let's suppose that you have highlighted this eight times in your achievements, so it looks pretty significant (by contrast, perhaps you have only used the word 'create' once). At this stage you may be able to say with some degree of certainty that you plan. The next question you need to ask yourself (by thinking back over your achievements) is *how* you plan. Some people like to set goals – they are very goal oriented. Some people are very good at taking a goal and thinking of a variety of ways to achieve it – they can strategize to create options for themselves. Others are more adept at working backwards from a clear end-point and thinking through the logistics involved in the task. Not everyone is motivated to plan or to plan in all the specific ways it is possible to plan. For example, someone may be excellent on strategy but poor on logistics – they can create all sorts of good options, but they need someone else with more practical gifts to work with them on the details of how something is going to happen. A word like 'organize' can suggest diverse ways of someone 'organizing' something. Similarly, words like 'decided', 'developed', 'managed', 'influenced' or 'communicated' *all* need significant 'unpacking'. *How* did you develop the idea? How *exactly* did you lead the team to victory? In *what way* did you influence her?

Step 4: Paying attention to 'sequences'

When you have 'unpacked' the words that are too generic – that is, when you have really discovered the *specifics* of what you 'do' in any given achievement – then it is important to understand that these activities fall into fairly predictable 'sequences'. To 'track' your strengths is to know what you always 'do' first, what you 'do' next and so on. We want you to group the activities you have found yourself describing around a series of four questions:

1   What were you doing when you first started the achievement?
2   What did you do to progress things as you moved through the achievement?
3   What did you do to deliver a result or get the 'job' done?
4   How did you bring the thing to a conclusion that was satisfying to you?

In other words, we want you to put the actions you went through in a sequence – 'I started by doing this and this, and then as I went on I did this and this … then I did this and this …' That should give you a sense of you 'in the flow'; you performing in a way that is 'natural' to you; you engaged in a set of activities that come easily for you. If you 'in the flow' is satisfying to you, this is the basis of your 'adding value' to your organization.

Turn to page 166 and order the verbs you have used into a sequence. The fourth question for you to answer there is: 'These activities seem to me to be ordered like this ...'

Step 5: Paying attention to 'the things that interest me'

So far we have looked at how you got started; what sustained you; and what you actually did (and in what order). Now we are going to look at what you were actually working with – the *subject matter* that is motivational for you.

Take the highlighter you have selected to represent the subject matter. Go back to your achievements and colour all the *nouns* that you use. For example:

- 'So I took the car and began by taking it to pieces very carefully. I made sure that I kept a note of the sequence, by putting each bit in a numbered pot.'
- 'My mum tested me on the words. I used to picture them in my mind.'
- 'I was angry with her. I mean, she had treated this man unfairly. I thought to myself, "This is a matter of principle."'
- 'I seemed to have a flair for display, I just seemed to know how to put things out so that they looked interesting.'
- 'Basically, the logistics of the party were down to me.'
- 'It was the sound of the words that I liked.'
- 'There's something brilliant about the feel of the water as you glide through it.'
- 'I am a fanatic when it comes to vegetables. I always go to the market myself to find the best.'
- 'As a kid I was always hanging around the base, so planes were part of my life.'
- 'When I had to tell Jack that his position was redundant I thought that would be the end of our friendship. But I

have kept in touch with him and still meet with him regularly.'
- 'I was aware that if we did what he suggested there would be a knock-on effect on the rest of the business – after all, we are all part of a system!'
- 'The group and I were all moving together now. It was great!'

Car, pieces, sequence, numbered pot, words, principle, display, look of things, logistics, sound of the words, feel of water, vegetables, planes, Jack, friendship, system, group! These are all examples of motivated subjects. The subject matter that is motivational to *you* is what you have written about, what you spend time talking about in your achievement stories. So highlight anything that looks like it was 'something' you were working with.

What have you found? In 'This Is Me At My Best' (where you have already filled in the answers to the first four questions) you will find that the next heading is 'This is what I like working with' (p. 167). Below it is a series of sub-headings:

- Intangibles
- Tangibles
- Data
- People
- Senses
- Mechanisms (i.e. means I use)

Using these as broad categories, transfer the lists of 'things' you have highlighted to page 167. If you find you have a lot of 'things' that seem similar (lots of people's names keep cropping up; planes, cars and ships all seem to recur; there are lots of examples of you travelling and sorting out timetables and maps; you keep on getting yourself into roles that require you to master special techniques), then see if you can think of a category that is more generic, such as vehicles, machines, gadgets, logistics, people as individuals, and groups of people. The subject matter that people write and talk about can be quite specific or quite general. We once worked with someone who had written eight achievements all about 'bell ringing' – so naturally we suggested that 'bells' were motivational to him. (Actually, when asked to expand on what he liked about 'bells', he also focused on the methodology of the art and the mathematics of ringing – so his motivated subject matter was much richer and wider than might seem at first sight!) See how you get on! Again, note the motivational significance of what you are experiencing now – if you like words, or data, or being methodical, or details you will find this exercise good. If you find detail tedious, go back to your favourite, crossword-loving best friend and plead with them again!

Step 6: Paying attention to 'results'

Now we have tracked what got you started; what kept you involved; what you actually did; and what you were actually working with. We haven't yet helped you to see the 'end point' for you. We have asked you to say *how* you delivered a result without looking to see what a 'good result' is *for you*. We need to do some more analysis.

Take your original highlighter pen (the one you have used already to mark the triggers and sustainers). We are now going to look for the 'endings' for you. At a certain point you achieve something, or your motivation seems to wane. You reached a point in all your achievements where you felt satisfied with what you did. What did that point look like? Some people focus on being able to handle or touch a finished product. Others find they get pleasure in being able to do something practical. Others feel satisfied when they hear the applause of the crowd. Some only feel satisfied when they have created a name for themselves. Some need to have a tangible reward like a certificate or a badge. Some aren't satisfied till they have some sort of position or status. Still others focus on the recognition they received from others. What were the common features of the 'ending' of your achievement *for you*? What *results* matter to you?

When you have highlighted anything that looks significant to you (the statements you have highlighted describe the *results* that you were looking for) compare what is highlighted with the following categories of results:

For you, does a 'good result' mean ...

- achieving a certain standard?
- seeing the goal or objective achieved?
- seeing the finished product?
- finding a practical application?
- achieving efficiency?
- saving some money?
- making some money?
- seeing the thing working well?

Or were there more 'human' dimensions to what gave you satisfaction? Dimensions such as ...

- being in front of audiences or viewers or listeners.
- being publicly visible.
- being able to enhance your reputation.
- the status that you enjoyed, the position that you reached.
- the awards, badges or trophies that you won.
- the support of others, which gave you the feeling that you had done well.
- the opportunity to be a bit different or distinctive.

This is *not* an exhaustive list. What other aspects of endings seem important in your stories?

What have you found now? Again, turn to 'This Is Me At My Best' (p. 168). The fifth question says: 'What results and recognition do I seek?' Write in all the phrases that you have just highlighted. List them each time they occur, and list them in their various forms (you may have used synonyms for the same result). Again, don't worry if you are not sure. *You* are the judge of how true the finished portrait is.

Still with us? Well done! You are well on the way to a really good understanding of your own motivation. The task of analysis will continue in the next chapter. What we have done in this chapter has been to look quite closely at the *mechanics* of what you have done (Steps 1–6 are all about the *details of how you work*). In the next chapter we will be looking at the bigger questions of the meaning of what you have done.

CHAPTER 5

More About Who You Are

Continuing to make sense of your story

I n Chapter 4 we started the process of analysis and accounting. We tried to 'track' your motivation and look for the 'flow' in it. In particular we 'tracked' what 'beginnings' look like for you; what the 'context' of your achievement looks like; what 'activities' you were engaged in, and in what 'order' you used your competencies; what things interested and motivated you; and we ended with what 'results' look like for you. So of the 10 Steps of the task of analysing and accounting, you have already completed Steps 1–6. Well done! Steps 7–10 are coming up soon. Let's remind ourselves of the Steps:

Step 1   Paying attention to 'beginnings'
Step 2   Paying attention to 'context'
Step 3   Paying attention to 'actions'
Step 4   Paying attention to 'sequences'
Step 5   Paying attention to 'what interests me'
Step 6   Paying attention to 'results'
Step 7   Paying attention to 'support'

Step 8   Paying attention to 'roles'
Step 9   Paying attention to 'meanings'
Step 10 Paying attention to how to tell your story!

In Chapter 4 we started the process of 'dissecting' the words and phrases of your achievements to see how they can be understood as having a structure. We have begun to see a 'pattern' to how you work when you are motivated. We have started the process of 'tracking' *your* process. We used a 'flow' diagram to represent this:

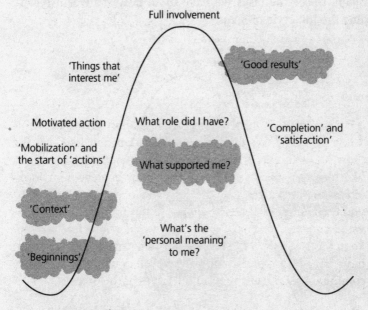

Figure 5i Overview of the 'flow' of an individual's motivation.

As you worked your way through Steps 1–6 (or persuaded a friend to do it for you!) you were following *how* achievement happens for you. We concentrated very much on the mechanics of you in action. What we have been trying to do is a bit like looking under the bonnet of a car to see how the engine works. Of course, some of what's under there is pretty obvious to you – after all, you've lived with yourself all your life! That's why we talked about not *discounting* your abilities in the last chapter. Your *differentiating* competencies are worth knowing and it's worth recognizing that they have a value in the workplace. What we are trying to do with you is to help you to become aware of how they work *together* to produce results that are satisfying to you and significant to others. The work we did in Chapter 4 has not completed what we can say about you 'in process'. This chapter should complete that task. Again, to see the tasks we have to do now, it's worth recapping the full cycle of Steps:

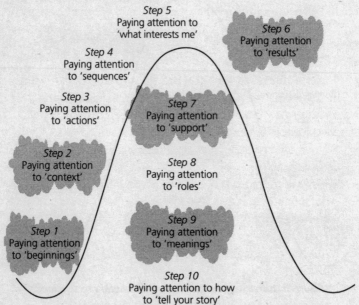

Step 5
Paying attention to 'what interests me'

Step 6
Paying attention to 'results'

Step 4
Paying attention to 'sequences'

Step 3
Paying attention to 'actions'

Step 7
Paying attention to 'support'

Step 2
Paying attention to 'context'

Step 8
Paying attention to 'roles'

Step 1
Paying attention to 'beginnings'

Step 9
Paying attention to 'meanings'

Step 10
Paying attention to how to 'tell your story'

Figure 5ii Overview of the steps of analysis and accounting.

In Steps 7–10 we are going to explore further what's 'under the bonnet', and then we will begin looking at the performance of the whole in context.

Step 7: Paying attention to 'support'

For most people achievement does not happen in a vacuum. Although there are some individuals of whom it is possible to say that their achievements really were exclusively done by them with *no* help from others, these are the rare exceptions. For most people, at some point in their achievement there is some support from somewhere. A critical step in this process is to understand what that support is. That is to say, your achievement stories, if you read them carefully, should enable you to answer the question: 'What supports me to give of my best?'

What support do you need in order to deliver the results we have been looking at in Step 6? What do we mean by 'support'? Let's give you some examples of things that people say to us:

- 'I was really at sea with the project until my boss helped me by giving me a sense of the "big picture".'
- 'I realize that when my room is in a mess it's really not good for me. I need order to function well.'
- 'She seemed to believe in me, and that made all the difference to me.'
- 'Knowing there was someone I could call at any point was what helped.'
- 'I realized early on that I needed to give myself time to prepare.'
- 'With my role clear, it seemed to make me much more effective.'
- 'What was most important to me was to have someone I could rely on to challenge my perfectionist streak.'
- 'Being left alone was probably the best thing that could have happened to me. It gave me time to experiment for myself.'
- 'Having someone around to whom I could give what I had done and have them progress it helped keep me on track.'

'Support' can be as simple as 'space to think', or as complex as having someone who is more expert than me to bounce ideas off and to work through the issues. And support can be something you need at a certain point of your process and no other. Knowing when you need support, knowing what that support needs to be and being able to find it when you need it could be the most significant piece of information you get from your achievement story.

If we use the flow diagram (Figure 5i, p. 91) as a guide, we can track the support you need over time. Do you need it at the beginning, but once you have had what you need there you don't need it elsewhere? Do you need it at the beginning and at certain key points during the process (at points of choice, when the circumstances change, if the goal-posts shift)? Do you need it only at the end when you've done your stuff?

Read through your stories and ask yourself what it is that is supportive to you in this achievement? When you think you have identified what you need and when you need it, choose a couple of people who know you well and, most critically, have been around you when you have been 'in full flow' (i.e. they have seen you during a time when you were undertaking your achievement), and ask them what they perceive about you and 'support'. Share with them the conclusions you have reached regarding where you see the key support issues in your achievements. When you have checked this out, turn to the 'This Is Me At My Best' section and under the question 'What supports me to achieve?' (p. 168) write a sentence that describes the support you need and the time when you need it.

Step 8: Paying attention to 'roles'

Step 7, looking at the 'support' question, may have raised some bigger questions for you – questions about your life in general. If it did, then that may be something that you need to pay attention to when, in Chapter 7, we ask you to plan actions to follow from your work in this book.

If you are still with us ... well done! Why don't you reward yourself now with something that will feel like you have patted yourself on the back? You are well over halfway through the 'analyse and account' part of the process! The next *three* steps are much more about how you can 'synthesize' from your story – how you can begin to get the 'big picture' from what you wrote.

Step 8 is a look at how you were operating *in relation to others*. Your achievements took place in the context of other people – even if your achievement happened entirely on your own and actively involved no one else! That 'people' context is the focus of Step 8. It's as if everything you did happened in a 'field' of other people. This Step attempts to explore the nature of how you are 'moving' with respect to those others. A few examples may help here. Please note that the examples below are phrases or sentences that people have used to describe themselves in relation to others:

- 'I suppose you would have to say that I was the one that made it happen ... being there in the middle meant that I could look after everything that came up.'
- 'Then it was my turn. There I was, completely on my own, racing against people who were much older than me. So when I won, it was great! I had done it all by myself. Naturally, I was pleased that my points contributed to the team, but at the end of the day it was my achievement.'
- 'When we danced it was like you couldn't see either of us. We were so together in the routine that the judges would have just seen the single entity.'
- 'I was the captain. I wasn't the best player but I kept the team pushing forward by my constant encouragement.'

- 'We were the sort of team that wanted to do everything together. We even had a set of shirts printed with our name on. We called ourselves "The A Team". We still meet up every now and then.'
- 'The bit I liked in the job was when I had to meet people and be the spokesperson for the company.'
- 'Without me they would never have done it. I used to go into their room and just "rev" them up. They needed someone with some energy to get them going.'
- 'I became their mentor. I met with them every month. I coached them through their problems and gave them the support they needed.'

Each of these statements describes someone who is occupying a different role in his/her relationship with the others in the achievement. Thus we have a person who wants to be key; an individualist; a really 'teamy' person; a team leader; another 'teamy' type; a representative; a catalyst; and a coach.

We could go on listing the plethora of ways in which it is possible for one person to 'relate' to others in an achievement. Remember, our task here is to look for the *consistencies*, to look for a pattern of repeated behaviour. We are *not* looking for the one-off occasion when you captained the side, or the one person you once gave advice to under the guise of a mentoring programme, or the one time when you had to lead a small group of people. We are trying to find examples of you operating in roles that you love doing. We are trying to find the one or two roles that are your *preferred* ways of relating to others. Some rare individuals can operate in a wide variety of roles, but most find that they have their own natural way of moving.

Now at this point we are conscious that what we are saying here may run counter to a lot of 'received wisdom'! That is to say, one of the most pervasive myths around today is that people can change their preferred way of operating with respect to others relatively easily – or if not easily, then at least with the application of some 'smart' technology (e.g. interactive video, CD-ROM, outward-bound-type courses, or some other 'advanced' technique). Educationalists, teachers, trainers, consultants, coaches, Human Resource Development types, personnel people, management gurus and personal development specialists all often appear to say that they can train anyone to do or be anything (with enough of the right resources!). Thus, if you learn a particular technique, or if you subscribe to a particular model, or if you practise the right set of 'habits', you will eventually become proficient and competent, and will have acquired the skills you need to do any number of quite diverse roles. Of course, people have an 'interest' in saying this – if you need to change, then you need a book, or a tape, or a training course, or a personal coach. What we are saying is that if you have a 'talent' to do something, then build on that – don't try to turn yourself into something that you are not. In contemporary society 'training and development' has become a catch-all. Just think of the number of times that politicians refer to it as 'the solution' to our problems. We call this a 'myth' because, in our experience over the last 35 years, we have not seen many clear examples of people 'developing' real ease and comfort about roles that go against their natural patterns of operating.

You may find that contentious. For now please suspend your judgement and see what the evidence from your story says.

Before you take your highlighter for this category, it might also be helpful for us to make some broad generalizations. We have found over the years that people, in describing their achievements, seem to fall into one of *three* general categories:

1 Some people's achievements focus on their particular contribution. They are satisfied by the activity itself, and their focus is less about how others are involved or can contribute. We call these people *contributors*. They may

contribute to the success of something, but their contribution is specific and defined. Their achievements are typically things that they did which involved their effort but not the effort of others (e.g. I won the race; I passed my driving test; I delivered a paper to the group; I became an expert in whatever, etc.).

2 Others find their satisfaction in being able to influence others in some way. They describe satisfaction in terms of how they were able to somehow affect others so that they were different as a result of the 'work' of the person. We call these people *influencers*. Influencers talk about the role they had in making a difference to others, but where there is little ongoing involvement with others. Influencers are often people with consummate people skills – they can build relationships, they can sell, they can negotiate, they can teach, they can sway a crowd. However, they want to affect others without necessarily being the ones with the overall responsibility. Influencers are often very good at getting jobs – even jobs they are *not* motivated to do. They can come across really well at an interview. They often end up working as consultants, teachers, coaches and so on.

3 There is a third group of people who don't just want to influence – they want to be responsible for others in a more sustained way. These are the people who *throughout* their achievements – from a very early age, right through till recent times – demonstrate a pleasure in overseeing others. We call these *leader/manager types*. It may be difficult to distinguish between someone who is exerting an influence in their achievement and someone who is taking on roles where there is a genuine interest in having an overall responsibility. Leader/managers want roles where they are responsible for others, where they have to let others achieve rather than achieving 'themselves'.

Take your highlighter pen and comb through your stories for phrases or sentences that speak about how you are relating to others.

What do the phrases you have found say to you about whether you are predominantly one type or another? As with the work in Step 5, we are going to give you some more help before you transfer the conclusions you are reaching to the 'This Is Me At My Best' section. As you look at your achievements, where is the focus of what you are doing? Some people like to relate to others when ...

- *they are starting something* – breaking new territory, pushing into the unknown, setting up something.
- *they are making a specific contribution to something* – performing themselves, actually doing the task themselves, giving something particular to others.
- *they are exercising some form of charisma* – they are the 'star', they are the catalyst, they are they real 'mover and shaker' of others.
- *they are focused on developing others* – they coach others or teach them, they find pleasure in the effect they can create in others.
- *they are linking others together* – they enjoy liaising between others, serving as a mediator or linchpin.
- *they enjoy getting the work or task done through others* – they like being in the midst of the people, coordinating the task, being at the centre of the action.
- *they work through some form of mechanism with respect to others* – they set up plans, they build blueprints and structures that others must conform to.
- *they are controlling others* – they like to monitor others, engineer outcomes for others.
- *they are in some position or have some status over others* – they need to be in a defined role of power or status with respect to others.

- *they enjoy leading or managing others* – they find satisfaction in getting others to do the work or the task, they actually want to have the responsibility for others.

Look at your own achievements. What do they indicate about how you relate to others? Look at the phrases or sentences that you have highlighted. What do they indicate about you? Stay close to this data. Don't start thinking about what you think you *ought* to be, or might like to be, or what others would like you to be! Stay with what your actual achievements are saying about how you seem to relate to others when you are at your best. Let your actual concrete experiences speak. Do they show you starting things with others? Are all your achievements about you and only you? Do they show you consistently creating contexts that have you being in front of an audience? Do they show you developing others? Do they show you bringing others together? Are the majority of your achievements full of examples of you being surrounded by others and achieving results through them? Do they reveal a controlling side to how you work? Are you always the one with the plan? Do your achievements show a concern with position and power?

If it is difficult for you to see any *consistent* pattern, try eliminating the options. Can you say with certainty that it is *not* a particular focus? If you can see no concern for power, or if you can see immediately that none of your achievements are about starting anything, or that you have no concern with having the 'limelight', then you can eliminate some of the categories easily!

Turn to the 'This Is Me At My Best' section and answer the question, 'What role/roles do I seem to take in my achievements?' (p. 169).

Step 9: Paying attention to 'meanings'

Describing how you relate best to others is the first of the really 'big' themes that we need to help you to see in your achievements. Step 9 gives us the next. We are trying to help you to see the hidden or latent meaning in the achievement to you. This is going to be hard because we don't want to *impose* meaning on your achievements in a way that is inappropriate. We don't want to 'box' you. Remember what we said about *not* type-casting you or fixing you in some limited system. That means that once again we must rely on letting your achievements speak for themselves. We must let the evidence that you have already prepared speak.

Take the last of your chosen highlighters. If the evidence is to speak for itself, you have got to let it. So what are we looking for? Motivational drives are difficult to describe. In some senses this step is tough because what we want you to do is almost a step back from the details of each achievement. We want you to take a 'helicopter perspective' on the achievement and ask yourself: 'If you were looking at this as an outsider, what would you say was the "essence" of this achievement? What do the words you have used about it say about what it means to you?' Thus, if we take an activity like 'passing my driving test', the number of ways in which it is possible to talk about 'passing my test' is legion.

Over the years, as we have worked with people's achievement data, we have found that people fall naturally into a broad set of categories. We are going to call these 'zones'. What do we mean by 'zone'? Experience has taught us that people's achievements show a certain focus. There are *five* significant foci:

Zone 1: Those who compare themselves to others
Some people, when remembering things that matter to them, when recalling their achievements, recall experiences or

events in which there is *always* some sort of comparison involved. Achievement to them is premised upon how they were in some sense differentiated from or compared to others. We say these people are in the *comparison to others zone*. Thus their achievements are peppered with a language of comparison – 'I was the best in the class'; 'My grade-point average was always better than my brother's'; 'I have always found a way of moving into the role that is the really critical one'; 'It was great because I was able to create a role for myself that was different from other people's'; 'The teacher wanted me to do it in one way, but I could see that I needed to do something unique' – and so on. People in this zone, if they were describing passing their driving test, would focus upon how significant it was for them that they were the *only* one in their family or class to do it, or the uniqueness of the way that they did it, or the fact that as a result of doing it they got to be the person in the group most in demand.

Zone 2: Those who focus on the process

Other people, in describing their achievements, don't focus on others in quite the same way. The language of their achievements is *not* peppered with lots of comparative comments. Rather, there is more of an emphasis on the *how* of what they did. These people remember, and describe in some detail, the *process* of what they were doing. These people are in the *process zone*. Thus their achievements are full of pleasure in the actual process that they went through as much as any particular result – 'I loved planning the holiday – there's nothing better than the feeling of anticipation coupled with poring over the maps'; 'I really enjoyed being in the dark room watching my pictures appear as if by magic in front of my eyes'; 'Progress is what matters to me – I find that if I know I am moving forward, then I'm OK'; 'Once I had built the first model I was hooked. I used to spend hours making them. It didn't really matter to me what happened to them once they were built.

I just loved making them.' People in this zone, in talking about the driving test, might focus upon the pleasure they got in the learning, or the sense in which passing the test for them was a milestone, or was an inauguration into adulthood, a rite of passage.

Zone 3: Those who seek defined ends

For others, such a preoccupation with process would drive them crazy. These are the people whose achievements are all discrete and defined. There is a strong sense of focus about what they have done. They are the sort of people who recall *specific* things that they have done, and for whom each achievement is pretty specific – I passed the test, reached the goal, delivered the result, climbed the hill, did what I had to do. These people are in the *defined purpose zone*. Thus, in their achievements they talk about what they did rather than how they did it; they talk of their pleasure in *having* done something; they feel good when they look back on what they have done – 'It was great that the party went so well'; 'Getting my test was the achievement'; 'Getting it right was what mattered to me'; 'Looking back, it was the challenge that interested me'; 'I couldn't rest till it was done – it drove me.' People in this zone, if they were talking about passing their driving test, would be clear that it was the challenge that mattered, or that they felt good that they got it right.

Zone 4: Those who focus on what effect they can have

Others have achievements that are full of descriptions of the effects that they were able to have. Such people describe their pleasure in influencing, or changing, or creating some sort of response in others. Not unnaturally, these people have often gravitated to roles where they can influence others or affect them – they have achievements as teachers, trainers, coaches, counsellors, supporters of others, and consultants. These people fill their achievement stories with tales of how much difference they made to others, how others' lives were affected by them. We describe these people as being in the *effect on the 'object' zone*. Thus they talk about significant encounters that they have where they help bring about change or help create an impression or elicit a response – 'I had the audience in my hand, I could do anything with them'; 'Helping my sister through her divorce was tough, but she was really grateful'; 'Supporting my mum through her illness made all the difference to her'; 'Getting the thing working was the real achievement'; 'I really enjoyed seeing the chest of drawers look good at the end'; 'Shaping the argument meant that we won the bid.' People in this zone, in describing passing their driving test, would describe how, as a result of the test, they could get more dates, or enhance their reputation, or become more popular, or astonish their parents.

Zone 5: Those whose focus is on some form of control or power

Last but not least, we have a group of people whose achievements reveal a pleasure in some sort of control or power that they have over something. This may not be overt and blatant, but in their language they reveal a concern with control, mastery, ownership, getting on top of something, beating the system, not being defeated, not giving up, overcoming, fighting, taking charge of something. We call such people those in the *power zone*. Thus their achievements are full of the language of mastery and control – 'I mastered the horse, it was not going to beat me'; 'We managed to win *despite* the fact that my finger was broken'; 'Not exploding with anger was the achievement'; 'I took control of the situation and shouted'; 'We were soaked, and by rights we shouldn't have carried on, but I kept pushing on'; 'I had cracked it, I had got my head round the thing.' People in this zone, in talking about passing their driving test, would focus upon the difficulties involved in doing it (they did it with a broken leg, or with a Force 10 gale!), or the power it gave them to control the vehicle, or the 'mastery' of the art of driving.

When you look at *your* achievements, and take what we described earlier as the 'helicopter' perspective – the outsider's view of the achievements – then you will begin to get a sense of how you might describe the 'essence' of your achievements in words. If you look at your achievements with a sympathetic and detached perspective, you should be able to say what the essence of each is. Thus, when you have determined what 'zone' your achievements occur in, it should also be possible for you to sum up the essence of what motivates you. For example, if *all* of your achievements involve you in exploring new things, pushing out from 'convention', going beyond what you are given, then you can be sure that you have a motivation in the 'process' zone (Zone 2), which is concerned with 'pioneering'. If your achievements are all about achieving specific targets, then you can be sure that you are in the defined-purpose zone (Zone 3), and you are motivated by the opportunity to meet challenges. If your focus is on what effect you had on someone or something, then you can be sure it is in Zone 4 – that is, effect on the object. People's motivational drives can be entirely focused in one zone, or maybe in a combination of two or three zones. They are never more than three. So your motivational drive may be in part about meeting a challenge, and in part about having an impact. All combinations are possible.

Take your highlighter and mark any phrase or statement that seems to speak about satisfaction, or to indicate where you find your pleasure in your achievements. Mark them and, using the descriptions above, by each of them put what zone the words seem to indicate. Again, if it is easier, use the method of elimination – this achievement is definitely *not* in the power zone, and so on. Having fixed for yourself the zone that you are in (remember that what zone you are in depends

upon where you focus your energies and what you get satisfaction from), then, by looking at the words you have used to
sum up the satisfaction you got in the achievement, it should
be possible for you to determine not just what zone you are in
but also to describe what satisfaction is *for you* in any achievement. This can take the form of a sentence that begins with
the phrase 'I want to ...' Your 'motivational pay-off', the drive
that runs through your achievements, is about your deep
wants, so being able to describe those in a sentence is important. These sentences will describe the 'essence' of the
achievement:

- 'I want to solve complex problems in order to fix things
  and make them work.'
- 'I want to turn ideas into visible end products.'
- 'I want to push myself, to prove I can do it, to pull it off.'
- 'I want to be central to projects and teams to help them
  deliver results.'
- 'I want to make an outstanding contribution and get
  recognition for it.'
- 'I want to find and exploit the potential in people, objects
  and places.'
- 'I want to make progress, advance, move on, keep moving
  forwards.'
- 'I want to serve people, meet their needs, do what they
  need.'
- 'I want to overcome difficulties in order to have an impact
  on people and events.'

Step 9 is complete if you have identified the zone that your
motivation falls into and you have developed a sentence for
yourself which describes the essence of what happens in your
achievements. If you turn to the 'This Is Me At My Best' section you can now complete the very last part of that: 'I find
satisfaction in ...' (p. 169).

When you have completed the section 'This Is Me At My Best' (with all the boxes of evidence complete with words and phrases) you can then transfer the conclusions to the summary beginning on page 170. This one-page summary should help you to see at a glance all the key themes of your motivation. It should give you a clear picture of who you are.

Sit back now and read through the whole of what you have done. Remember what we said right at the beginning of this process: *you* are the best 'expert' in your own material. You are the judge of whether what you have done represents 'you at your best'. If it doesn't, then the chances are that you need some help, you need someone to give you some support in this process. We haven't finished the whole process yet, but we are very close. So if what you have managed to do so far feels stilted, or feels incomplete, stop for a bit, have a coffee or tea and then come back to the task when you have recovered your energy. Then, go back to Step 1 and do the whole exercise again.

Step 10: Paying attention to how to tell your story

Step 10a

We are in the home straight now! Step 10 brings the whole thing together. Take what you have done in the 'This Is Me At My Best' section. This is your 'working document'. It's probably full of scribbles and false starts. Don't worry. It's good to know that you have been working hard at this. Now we are going to try to tidy this up so that you can use what you have created. This is important. What you have before you is a set of information that is 'bitty', disjointed, entirely 'you-focused'. What we need to do in this step is to turn it into something that communicates to others. We have got to get you to the point where *you* can communicate it to others. We do this in *two* ways: firstly by getting you to draw out your motivation on the 'flow cycle'; and secondly by rewriting the whole thing as a set of flowing words, as a story of your own – we call this your *ideal job*.

Drawing your motivation out as a flow will create something that looks like this:

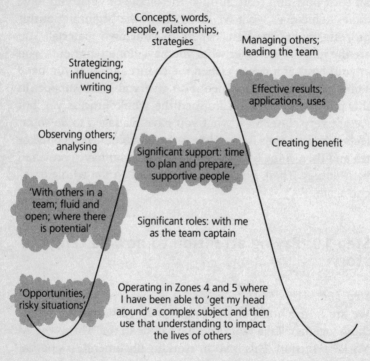

Figure 5iii Overview of Nick's motivation showing how the 'flow' happens.

Or it might look more elaborate and may use pictures as well as words:

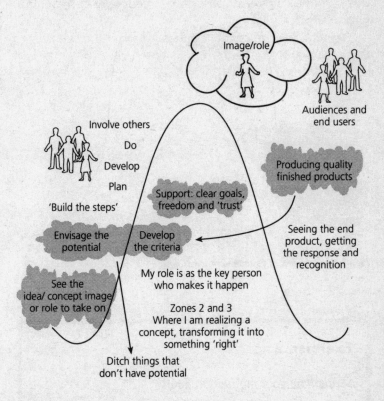

Figure 5iv Overview of the 'flow' of a person's motivation using words and pictures.

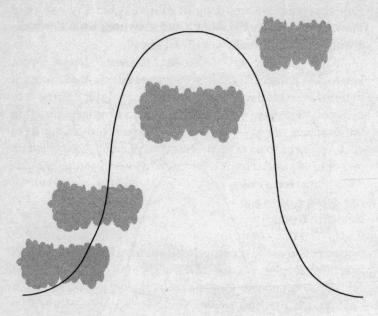

Figure 5v Overview of your motivational flow.

Exercise 8

Seeing how your motivation flows

Take the information you have written in the 'This Is Me At My Best' section and map it as a flowing sequence on the blank curve given in Figure 5v. This should take you a good 40 minutes.

Note that what we are trying to do here is to tell the story of 'how I am motivated' – what gets me started; what keeps me going; what I'm actually doing and so on.

Telling your story is the essence of the *second* thing we want you to do – namely, to construct a way of talking about yourself in terms of an ideal role or job. The purpose of this exercise is to help you to prepare yourself to be able to describe yourself in 'motivational' terms – something that can have value as part of what you need to do to prepare a good CV and to be able to talk meaningfully and informatively about yourself and your motivations at career review meetings and selection interviews. We can picture this task and the eventual goal like in the way shown in Figure 5vi.

The first thing to do in establishing how you can communicate who you are to others is to move away from your portrait as an abstract piece of paper to a fruitful understanding of what sort of role or job you should be looking for. As you do this, it is important that the pattern you have identified should be understood and used as an integral system of strengths and motivations. Do not make the mistake of extracting from your pattern *one* element and generalizing this beyond the other modifying elements.

For example, if the pattern you have found includes a strength in investigating by surveying and gathering general information, don't think that this inevitably points you into a job involving *nothing but* surveying. Look at how the surveying relates to other aspects of the pattern – that is, under what circumstances and to what end? An interest in investigating might imply that you should be involved in a marketing function, but other aspects of your motivation would also need to point in that direction.

It is only as you *integrate each element* with other elements that any one part can be properly understood.

However you want to look at it, the way you outline your ideal job or role description is to synthesize the elements of the

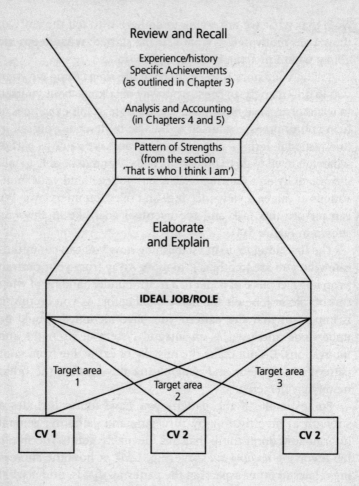

Review and Recall

Experience/history
Specific Achievements
(as outlined in Chapter 3)

Analysis and Accounting
(in Chapters 4 and 5)

Pattern of Strengths
(from the section
'That is who I think I am')

Elaborate
and Explain

IDEAL JOB/ROLE

Target area
1

Target area
2

Target area
3

CV 1   CV 2   CV 2

Figure 5vi Overview of the ideal job/role exercise.

pattern you have drawn out from your achievements into a single, extended and elaborated statement. The 'flow' can follow what you have already done. This is a more narrative style.

Step 10b

Using the categories you have written in the section 'This Is Me At My Best', construct an ideal job or role description using your own words. Please note that the pattern of strengths you have found was produced by *abstracting* from the raw data. In this part of the exercise you need to put back into the abstract or general the *particulars* and *specifics* that motivate you. That is, you need to describe just what sort of people or ideas or things or contexts you want to work with.

An ideal job or role would involve me working with ...
(Insert the things that appear in your subject matter [from Step 5 above] and illustrate them – e.g. 'I enjoy working with tools, both conceptual and practical, like spreadsheets.')

where the conditions of work were ...
(Insert the elements that describe the ideal circumstances or context [from Steps 1, 2, 6 & 7 above] for you to work in – e.g. 'I find it fun to be involved with people who enjoy interaction and mucking in, where I get support from my boss.')

and where I could operate with others in the following ways ...
(Insert in your own words the phrase used in the relationship section [from Step 8 above] and add ways in which that would find expression in particular roles – e.g. 'fact finder', 'resources person', 'database king'.)

using my motivated abilities to ...
(Describe them as a sequence/process [from Steps 3 & 4
above] – e.g. 'Where I can analyse a problem in order to
structure a solution so that I can write reports.')

and which leads to ...
(Insert the phrases from your essence/pay-off [your central
motivational thrust from Step 9 above] – try to capture
them in your own words.)

Step 10c

Rewrite your ideal job or role description so that it flows smoothly, emphasizes those things that are *most* important to you, and is in your own words. Put it aside and come back to it later. Does it need another rewrite?

If you're not *really excited* about what you've just described, then it's not your ideal job/role! Try working on it some more. Below is an example of a well-written 'ideal job'!

My ideal job is one where ...

... I can *make/build* something – to be in at the early stages, embryonic, a time of significant growth. I like *managing the change from the beginning (concept, idea) through the middle (planning, empowering others) to the end (final result, lasting impact)*. I want to push back boundaries of my own knowledge – I like new challenges (technological, new methodologies, new tools and techniques). Not necessarily the leading edge, but bringing new technology, processes and techniques *to an entity which lacks them*.

... a *need* for growth/change is present. I develop sufficient understanding of the technology, approach etc. in order to formulate a concept (or several concepts) which meets the need. The concept must have the potential for a *lasting* benefit to somebody or some process. I like to take nebulous ideas (from myself or others) and put some structure into those ideas – conceptualizing in a *picture*, testing the perceived benefit/value, *anticipating* pitfalls, evaluating *risk*, charting the course, *evaluating* alternative courses, recognizing where they might lead, and discarding or *modifying* the original concept.

... once a strategy is developed, I ensure that everything that should be covered is being covered, and that *monitors and controls are in place* so that people can monitor themselves against the mileposts, preferably in a *visual* format. When adjustments/ modifications need to be made, ensuring that they are consistent with the original design intent.

... in bringing about changes which will have a lasting beneficial effect/impact, I anticipate people's actions and reactions to technological change, putting myself in their situation, *thinking through how best to involve them in the change in a way that empowers them*, pushing decision-making down in organizations. For example, by giving people information very early in a project so that they get used to the idea and can add value where appropriate.

... I can understand the process that I'm involved with, by gathering data and facts, investigating the overall process, or even manually learning how it works. When

appropriate, I enjoy sharing my knowledge with others by showing or demonstrating and then encouraging the person to *run with it*!

... I know people as *individuals*.

... I will receive recognition for my role in bringing about the change – especially from the individuals whom I have influenced/guided/shaped, who are now equipped in ways they weren't before. I like to know that I have used *my gift of enabling/facilitating* to bring about a lasting beneficial change to the business and the people who are part of it.

CHAPTER 6

How to Avoid Getting 'Stuck'

How to keep yourself from being stressed and how to stay 'in the flow'

If you have completed everything we have asked you to do in Chapter 5, then you are at a point where the nature of who you are should be a little clearer to you. In this chapter we want to help you to *use* what you have found out about yourself in Chapters 4 and 5. There are *two* things we want to help you to do.

First, we want you to understand the points or the places when your motivation doesn't 'flow' – we want to help you to see the times when you get 'stuck' and to see the causes of that problem.

Secondly, we want to help you to see how you can use the new understanding of yourself in *all* areas of your life – particularly those areas where you have 'issues' (this could be frustration at work, or conflict at home, or uncertainty about the future). In all probability it could be the very reason you picked up this book. Do you remember that we asked you to complete an exercise right at the outset of this book (see Exercise 1, p. 11)? Why did you start reading this book? What did you hope to get from the book? What has kept you going through all the hard work of the 'analysis and accounting' phase? If we can, we want to help you to use the insight you have gained to revisit that central concern.

Avoiding getting 'stuck'

'Getting stuck' – not exactly a technical term, is it? Not exactly a precise scientific description of a psychological state! Still, it's pretty graphic, isn't it? We spend the majority of our time working professionally with people who have got 'stuck' and who don't know how to get themselves 'unstuck'. 'Stuckness' is when your motivation has come to an end, or when your motivation isn't getting you what you want, or when no matter what, you just can't seem to break out of a negative pattern of doing but not getting the results you want. Here are some of the things that people say to us about their lives:

- 'My career seems to have petered out. I don't seem to be getting anywhere!'
- 'I deliver the results but others take the credit, and others get offered better chances.'
- 'I know I can do it, but I just don't seem to be able to get others to see that I can.'
- 'I've got no confidence in myself. I'm petrified that next time I won't be able to do it again.'
- 'I know I'm not in the right job. My tiredness and my lack of motivation tell me that. But I've got no idea what I should be doing!'
- 'I can do it, but it's at such a cost to me!'
- 'I've lost the blueprint – I don't know what's next!'
- 'I don't have anything to offer. I don't have the right skills, the right education, the right connections, the right support …'

However people express it, they are describing the state of 'being stuck'. Now the people who said these things are not 'duffers', they are not people who are 'unsuccessful'. These are often very successful people. They are people who have achieved a great deal, who have done some pretty amazing things. It's just that they have reached a point where they say they have come to a halt. That's 'stuckness'. That's the place where a person's 'flow' has dried up, where their self-renewing capabilities have failed. Do you know that feeling? Have you reached that point before? Are you at that point now?

'Flow' is the opposite of 'stuckness'. What we were helping you to chronicle in Chapters 4 and 5 was a view of you 'at your best' – when everything worked for you so that you were able to perform at your best. Not all contexts or circumstances will give you that opportunity. Being aware of what attracts you and supports you is the *first* step to being able to shape your life accordingly. So being able to describe your ideal job or role is a good first step. Similarly, being able to 'track' yourself in your achievements is equally a good step. Both of these positive ways of looking at yourself can be helpful in providing you with a set of criteria to look at options and determine whether what's available to you meets the criteria *that matter to you motivationally*. For example, if, from the work you have done so far, you can say with certainty that your achievements show that you like new things, that are *challenging* and where there is scope to develop, then any role that does not include these as central will be tedious to you (thus routine and maintenance are out!). Your ideal job or role can be 'converted' into a set of criteria. The more any role or option *maximizes* the criteria that matter to you, the better it's going to be for you.

Developing criteria for me to identify 'best fit' jobs or roles

Let's see how we can 'convert' what you have found out about yourself into a grid that you can use to 'screen' possibilities and options. Turn back to what you did right at the end of Chapter 5 (we are going to use part of the work in Step 10b on page 114). Using your achievement data, you found a set of words to describe the 'conditions of work' or the 'context' (these are the ideas that you had previously generated in Steps 1, 2, 6 and 7 earlier in the chapter). These are the aspects of your motivation that appear in the 'flow' diagrams (Figures 4ii, 5i and 5iii are marked with grey 'clouds'!). In Exercise 9 we'd like you to do the following:

1 Take each of these words and, in the boxes provided, put them on one or the other end of the scale (you will see that we have put in a couple of examples).
2 On the other end of the scale think of the most *opposite* circumstance you can (e.g. in a team – by myself; where there is pressure – where there is no pressure; a visible role – hidden away; with me as an expert – where I don't really have to 'know' much; where objective standards matter – where you can make things up as you go along, etc.).
3 Now take the way that you described the role that suited you best (i.e. what you found out about yourself in Step 8 in Chapter 5) and do the same with it (e.g. where I'm encouraging others – where I have to reprimand them; where I am leading others from the front – where I am just one of the troops; where I am monitoring the people as we go along – where I have no control, etc.).
4 Finally, take the aspect of your motivation that describes the 'meaning' to you (i.e. what you found in Step 9 and described in Step 10b) and do the same with it (e.g. where

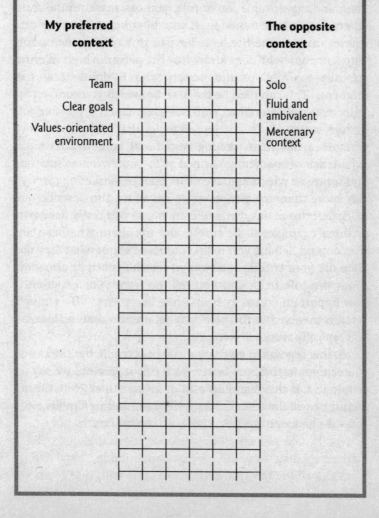

Exercise 9

Creating the criteria for me

Converting the elements of the 'context' that are
motivational to me into criteria to evaluate a role or option

My preferred context						The opposite context
Team						Solo
Clear goals						Fluid and ambivalent
Values-orientated environment						Mercenary context

I am in control – where I have no control; where I am making a difference – where I have no influence, etc.).

Note that down one side of the box there should be a set of words that describe what we might call a 'pig in mud' scenario for you. Down the other side there is the 'scenario from hell' for you! Give this half an hour.

Then, for any possible job or role, you can mark on the scale where the job/role would fit. If you don't know, then the categories can become the basis for you to have a conversation with someone who does know (say the person who is offering you the job/role, or the person who is doing it at the moment). This can then be the basis on which you conduct an 'informational interview' with someone about a possible job or role option. Let's say, for example, that you don't know whether a role in marketing would suit you. You have no experience of marketing. Armed with your criteria, you can find someone who does have experience of marketing (preferably more than one person, since we all tend to describe our work in terms of our own motivation – so you really need two or three examples to be sure!), and ask them whether they would mind helping you to find out more about what they do. Then use your criteria as a basis on which to elicit information about the role (e.g. 'Can you tell me from your experience how important creativity is in a role like yours?' 'How much detail is involved in this role?' 'What are the time-scales that you typically work to?' etc.).

No role is going to give you a 100 per cent fit, but the closer you can get to that, the better. As a rule of thumb, we say to people that if they can find a fit of greater than 70 per cent, then they will find themselves well suited and well motivated, and the chances of getting 'stuck' will be minimized.

When the flow gets interrupted

'Stuckness' is not simply about gross mismatch in the context. It can be much more subtle than that. What can be particularly helpful is to understand where and how the motivational 'flow' gets interrupted. Let's take the person whose 'flow' chart we described at the end of Chapter 5:

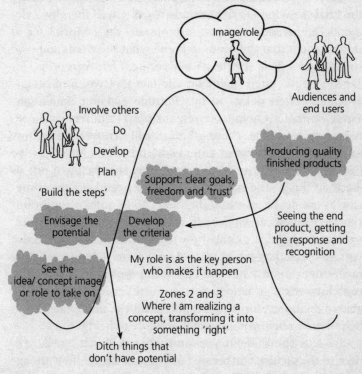

Figure 6i Overview of the 'flow' of a person's motivation using words and pictures.

As we have said, this picture represents this person when everything is working for her – this is her at her best. Where might a person such as this find that flow gets stopped?

It's a difficult question to pose in the abstract! However, two things strike us about this person as we look at the flow. The critical steps for her concern 'being able to envisage the outcome' – that incredible moment when she sees what the end-point is going to be (what we have represented here as the 'cloud' with the picture of her in an image or role); and 'getting it right' – her need for clear criteria of 'quality' (what we have represented in the diagram with the arrow linking the final grey cloud to the second grey cloud). If these two elements, for whatever reason, are absent, she's 'stuck'! It's at that moment that she needs to know what she needs and who she can get it from (her boss? her partner? her mentor?).

'Stuckness' often highlights the fact that we need others. Stuckness often points to our finitude and our limitations. Those limitations help us to see our need of others with *complementary* strengths. Those others need to know from us how they can help. Most of us don't want indiscriminate help – we just need a nudge or a little something that helps to put us 'back on track'. The specifics of how we need help are as specific as the details of us 'in the flow'. To be able to communicate to others what we need from them is a great step forward.

'I'm stuck, I don't know how to move from here! Can I use you as a sounding-board? Can I ask you to help me get clear in my own mind what the end result would look like? I'm conscious that I'm helped if I can have clear criteria.' To be able to ask others for their support and help, and to be able to help them to help you is a great antidote to being 'stuck'.

So, let's think about you and what gets you 'stuck'. Go back to the picture you created of yourself 'in the flow' in Figure 5v (p. 110). Exercise 10 is for you to find out the ways that you get 'stuck'.

1 Take the picture that you drew of yourself 'in the flow' in Figure 5v (if possible blow it up on a photocopier so that you have more space to write more).
2 Think of four or five occasions when things weren't going

well for you, when you were definitely not 'at your best'. Picture yourself in the context. What was it about those circumstances that wasn't working for you? Looking at yourself in the 'flow' diagram, can you identify the point or points where you got 'stuck'? In the boxes provided write down the things that happened and the way you think got 'stuck'.

3 'Stuckness' can emerge from two sources: you get stuck either because of what *you don't do but should*, or because of what *you do do but shouldn't* – by way of analogy, what we might call 'sins of omission' and 'sins of commission'! What you don't do but should are really those aspects that need to be done but which you are not motivated to do. For example, you might not be good at detailed planning, and logistics bore you, so every time you get mobilized you really ought to do some scheduling, but because other aspects interest you more you don't give the time to careful planning. Consequently things begin to fall apart as the project matures. What you do do but shouldn't are all the things you do to excess. For example, you may be motivated by the pleasure of 'maximizing' your time and resources, but your 'maximization' motivation, if unchecked, can put the whole enterprise in jeopardy if you miss a deadline. The 'Who Do You Think You Are?' process has been created to help you build a portrait of yourself at your best – a picture of your strengths. But your strengths aren't everything. You have weaknesses too – the things that you are not motivated to do but are required to do (e.g. you may be a great batsman, but if the game needs bowlers you are at a disadvantage!); and, most critically, at least in our experience, the things in your motivation that you do to excess. Your 'weaknesses' get you stuck either because you ignore something that isn't of motivational significance, or because you focus so much on some aspect of real motivational significance to you that, again, you miss the wider implications.

What about you? Take time now to complete Exercise 10. Give this 30 minutes.

Exercise 10

Times and contexts when I got stuck

Time 1

Time 2

Time 3

Time 4

As you think about yourself in context, it may help you to think of how your motivation overlaps with your existing job (if you have one) or role (choose any context where you function in relation to others – e.g. as a parent or a sibling). Picture your motivation and your context as two 'sliding boxes' that can overlap to varying degrees:

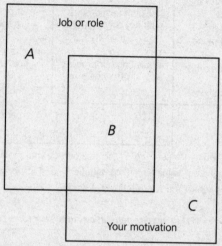

A represents those requirements of the job that you are *not motivated to do.*
B represents those motivated abilities you have that *are* required for the job, what we call 'good fit'.
C represents those motivated abilities you have that are *not* required for the job

Figure 6ii Overlap of your motivations and your role.

How close is the fit for you? Remember the rule of thumb – a 70 per cent fit is good! Overleaf is an example of someone who has completed these boxes.

A Poor fit for me	B Good fit for me	C Poor fit for me
(because I am expected to perform tasks that I am *not* motivated to do)		(because I can't use these strengths in the role)
•	•	•
Project management where I have to handle all the logistics of the project	researching new markets and identifying trends	not got full 'P&L' responsibility
•	•	•
dealing with money	building relationships with key players in the market	no chance to produce finished products
•	•	•
monitoring the office	innovating our product offerings	no outlet for my interest in performance
•		

A   Things you do (or don't do) in the area outside your motivation

B   Sources of real 'value added' contribution, good fits for you

C   Areas in which you are unfulfilled at work

Figure 6iii Overlap of your motivations and your role (example).

What happens to people when there is little real overlap – that is, when there are large aspects of your role or job that you are not motivated to do, or when a significant number of your motivations aren't used by the job or role? Each of us has a variety of mechanisms (or, indeed, non-mechanisms) to cope with this. A positive mechanism would be to pour ourselves into activities in a different context – if work 'sucks', we can always run the local residents' association, or coach the boys' football team, or lead a church house-group, or live for our non-work life. A non-mechanism would be simply to ignore it, to hope that it's just a passing phase, to deny that you are 'stuck' and then to live with the consequences.

Exercise 11

Mapping my motivation and my context

Choose a role that you are required to perform (e.g. your
current job, your role at home, your role in your church)
and map the things that fit well and those where there are
serious 'misfits'. Give this exercise 30 minutes.

A Poor fit for me
(because I am expected
to perform tasks that I am
not motivated to do)

-
-
-
-
-
-

B Good fit for me

-
-

-
-
-

C Poor fit for me
(because I can't
use these
strengths in the
role)

- **A** represents those requirements of the job/role which you are *not motivated to do* but which you have to do in order to do the job.
- **B** represents those aspects of motivation you have which *are* required for the job – what we call 'good fit' (remember that we are aiming for 70 per cent good fit).
- **C** represents those aspects of motivation you have which are *not* required for the job but which are motivational to you. What happens to them at present?

What are *your* preferred means to deal with the aspects of yourself or your role that are 'out of kilter'? Are there any better alternatives for you that are feasible at this time (bearing in mind the constraints that you face)?

Perhaps the boxes are too static for you to really get a handle on your context and its fit for you. Perhaps we need a more dynamic metaphor or image. The next section is another way of looking at you 'in context'.

Looking at you 'in context' – understanding your place in 'the system'

We help lots of people who are in 'conflict' in some way. 'Stuck' people are in conflict with themselves; 'stuck' people end up in conflict in teams; and 'stuck' people are often in conflict with their organization. People 'get out of kilter' with themselves and with their surroundings – especially with the other people in their various worlds. Helping them to see themselves as part of a complex system can often be the first step towards real change and improvement. The following exercise is one way of picturing what's going on and of trying to make sense of it. It is an attempt to bring a 'systems approach' to you in context. Peter Senge, the man who has done most to popularize the notion of systems thinking in business recently, describes a system as a 'perceived whole whose elements "hang together" because they continually affect each other over time and operate toward a common purpose'. On that definition virtually anything can be seen as a system – a partnership, a team, an organization, an organization in a marketplace, the collection of organizations that service a particular market. For our purposes here we would like you to do some work on 'you at work' as a system. (If you would prefer to apply this learning to something outside work – e.g. to you in your relationship with your 'significant other', or you in your family – please feel free to go ahead.)

This exercise is a little like the one you did in Chapter 3 – that is to say, you need to do it, and *then* let it speak to you.

1 Choose a situation you are in that is in some senses *not* working for you (e.g. a team you are part of, your place in the company, your relationship with another group, your relationship with your boss – in short, any situation you are in where there is more than just you involved and where it's far from ideal for you). If doing this in abstract is hard for you, think of an example of something at work that really 'bugs' you, and start working with that as your scenario.

2 Identify who is involved in this – both those who are directly involved and those less directly involved (e.g. this story directly involves me, my boss, my colleague and, indirectly, our customers).

3 Identify what it is about the current situation that is *not* working for you, and which you would like to see changed as a result of this work. Like the exercise you have just done on 'stuckness', this may link back to Exercise 1 (p. 11) which we asked you to do at the beginning of the book. Why are you motivated to work

through a book on identifying your strengths? What is it about your current situation that makes you in some senses so dissatisfied with your life that you are reading 'self-help' books in your spare time?

4 If it would help you to recall in detail what is going on, then in narrative form write down what's happening to you as you see it. Use the following questions as a guide to jog your recall. You might try to describe your context by recalling a specific incident that is 'typical' of what's happening to you. Who is involved in it – directly and indirectly? What actually happens – how do things unfold? What do you see, hear, observe, note, smell? What do you experience? What do you think? What do you feel? What else are you aware of? Does this happen often? What do you want to happen? What does the other party/person want? How does it normally finish? Does anything happen after that to you or to the other party?

5 Find a quiet place where you can work comfortably on a flat surface. This exercise is meant to help you to 'reframe' what is going on for you. It will probably take about 30 minutes to do it well.

6 Take a large piece of white paper (A4 paper will do, but A3 paper would be better, and flip-chart paper would be ideal).

7 Gather together a collection of coins (give yourself maximum flexibility by getting at least one £2 coin, four £1 coins, four 50p pieces, six 20p, five 10p, six 5p, six 2p and ten 1p).

8 Take out the coins you have collected. These are going to be used as 'symbols' to help you describe to yourself the situation *as you see and experience it*. The sheet of paper is the context/arena in which what you want to explore is occurring. Choose coins to represent each of the 'players' in the system. Put them in an appropriate place on the

paper and write on the paper what's going on for you. Feel free to move the coins as you see fit and/or to change them or add to them if the story you are telling yourself demands a change. The fact that you can move them, change them, add to them and take them away is important – systems are dynamic, things go through phases and change over time. The coins are there to help you to see the *dynamics* of the process you are involved in. The value of the coins can have meaning too – choosing to represent a person with a £1 coin rather than with a 50p can be symbolic. Not that this is a precise exercise – what we are trying to do is to get you to see yourself 'in context'. This is your chance to retell the story of 'you in context' and to see how things link together *for you*, or *not* for you, as the case may be. What does retelling it using the coins tell you?

We have created a mini-scenario in Figure 6iv overleaf, for you to see what we mean by this.

If this exercise seems silly and you aren't getting much from it, try the same exercise with a friend. Ask your friend to help you to see the situation from a new perspective. Pay particular attention to how it is *now* and how *you would like it to be*. What does the difference tell you? What would it take for what you want to actually happen?

9 Once you have seen the situation for yourself afresh using the coins, try to express what you have seen in words. When you first chose the coins to represent the various players, what did that tell you? When you set the coins on the piece of paper, what did the positioning of the coins tell you about how you feel in your current role? What did the various movements of the coins represent? What does the difference between where you are now and where you would like to be tell you? Let the coins speak to you! Let the coins tell you what you haven't been

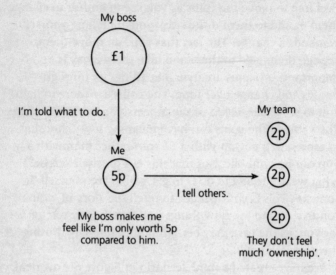

How it is *now*

My boss

£1

I'm told what to do.

My team

2p

Me

5p ——————————> 2p

I tell others.

My boss makes me
feel like I'm only worth 5p
compared to him.

2p

They don't feel
much 'ownership'.

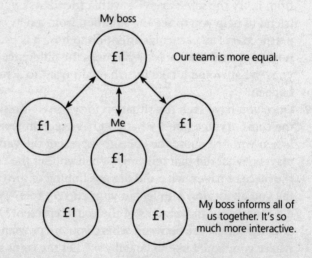

How I'd like it to be...

My boss

£1

Our team is more equal.

£1   Me   £1

£1

£1   £1

My boss informs all of
us together. It's so
much more interactive.

Figure 6iv Using the coins exercise to see yourself in context.

seeing about your current context. Listen to the subtle signals in your story about you in context.

10 Go back to the description you wrote of your ideal job (in Chapter 5, p. 116). Compare what you have written about your current context as a result of this exercise. What does it indicate to you? Looking at your current context, how good is the 'fit' between what you are motivated to do (and how you are motivated) and the demands of your job/context? Remember that we have found over the years that people who are in roles where there is a fit of greater than 70 per cent by and large are fairly comfortable with themselves and their work. Anything less than that, and the situation indicates that some radical adjustment may need to take place. How about you? What do the coins tell you?

If you are to avoid getting stuck, you have to know how your own 'process' – your own 'flow' – works, and you have to know how to see yourself as part of a system. Then you need to set about making the necessary changes. That is the subject of our last chapter.

CHAPTER 7

Where Next?

*Knowing who I am
and what I should
be doing now*

In Chapter 6 we were encouraging you to use the information you had discovered about yourself in Chapters 4 and 5 to reflect back on your immediate context. We moved into 'listen and learn' mode. In this chapter we want to think about helping you to take some action. Actually, given what we have already been working on in looking at how your motivation 'flows', it should be easy for you to say the conditions or context that you need to become motivated. Let's start by going right back to what you wrote in Exercise 1. We asked you to put down what you wanted to get from working through this book. Now as we reach the 'home stretch', have we been helping you to achieve what you wanted? As you work through this chapter, bear in mind what you wanted, and prepare to make changes in the light of what you have learnt.

It's never too soon and it's never too late to make changes in your life. That doesn't mean it is easy to begin a change process. But if there is one great feature about life at the end of the twentieth century and the beginning of the twenty-first century, it is simply the fact that making changes to your life career is more possible now than it has been for many people in past generations. Change is not the property of a privileged few.

It is possible to be cynical about how often company directors and management gurus mouth that 'people are the most important asset of the company', and there can sometimes be an uncomfortable amount of truth in Scott Adams's *Dilbert* cartoon. However, organizations that mobilize people's gifts and strengths, and that don't just give lip-service to it, do better for everyone. As Peter Drucker, that guru of gurus, has observed: 'Effective management is the productive use of strengths'. Getting this right – of really knowing how to 'empower' people to give of their best and make their contribution – will, we believe, be the single most important differentiator of successful companies. Enabling people to shape their roles to maximize their contribution so that they can reach for the best that they can be has become a key theme in the life of many *progressive* companies. Donald Peterson, the former chairman and Chief Executive Officer of the Ford Motor Company, is quoted as saying: 'It appears possible that a permanent culture change has occurred at the Ford Motor Company emphasizing the importance of people and empowering them. If this should happen, it will be the greatest accomplishment in my professional life.'

All that you have learnt about yourself from the exercises in this book will be of little value if it is not directly applied to your life situation. So how might you go about making the change? Here are *seven* vital steps in your personal action plan.

1. Owning the change

Firstly, go back to one of the first exercises you did in this book – the one with the clouds, where you had to put down some of the things that you are dreaming of (Exercise 2, p. 26).

What do those dreams tell you about yourself? What sort of changes were you looking to make as a result of working through this book to address the question of who you are? As you have worked through the book, what else has emerged? In the last chapter, what did the coins tell you about your situation? Did they point to the need to make some changes? What about the sliding boxes exercise (Exercise 11, p. 131)? What did the process of mapping your motivation against your job or role tell you? How much do you need to make some key changes in the way you live your life? Two other key indicators may be important:

First, in listing your achievements, has it been easier to identify key achievements that took place some years ago, or have you been able to make lists of recent achievements? It doesn't require much imagination to realize that if your achievement list has run dry in recent years, this may well indicate a degree of 'stuckness' that calls out for change.

Secondly, in reviewing any recent changes, have these all been within your work, or are you discovering that your achievements are mostly outside of your paid employment? Clearly, the more that your major accomplishments fall outside of the workplace, the greater the requirement that there might be for change.

If it is becoming clear to you that making a change is an important consideration, then you need to take on board the following commitments:

No one else will make the change for you. It is your responsibility, and only yours, to take the initiative in producing change.

Change is costly. You will need to consider the extent to which the changes you make will impact the lives of those around you.

The cost of change is effort and work. Making significant change will require work on your part, and it is worth asking whether you value your future life-pattern enough to make that investment of effort.

The cost of change is time. There are major time implications attached to making change. Setting aside the time to review your options may well require some immediate changes in your work/leisure pattern. All too often life changes are avoided precisely because people are caught in a pattern of unrewarding work which makes such huge time demands that there is no time left over to invest in reviewing change options.

Beware of the velvet rut! The single biggest change inhibitor tends to be the velvet rut – the well-paid job that we don't particularly like but which finances a comfortable lifestyle. As John F. Kennedy once observed: 'There are risks and costs to any programme of action but they are far less than the costs of comfortable inaction.'

2. What changes do I want?

In Chapter 6 we talked about job fit. A necessary goal to produce a satisfying working experience is to produce a high level of job fit (remember our rule of thumb: 70 per cent is good). But what if that is not possible? Essentially there are four potential changes that you can evaluate.

Make the job better
George was an excellent trainer for the telecommunications company that he worked for. Over a number of years, he became aware that he was increasingly looking to his leisure time as a means of providing fresh challenges and achievements. His work had become boring. There were still aspects of his job that interested him, especially meeting new people, and trying new techniques in the training courses that he organized. But somehow that was not enough.

As George's self-understanding grew, he realized that a key motivating factor for him was the ability to 'pioneer'. In the past he had pioneered aspects of the training programme for his company, but now that the training needs of the company were well served, he had gradually lost interest. Simply updating the courses was not enough. He needed a new challenge.

After discussion with his boss, his training brief was changed. He was still in charge of training, but the day-to-day maintenance of the courses was managed by someone else. George was given the additional task of finding completely new courses, new ways of training, and of bringing a cutting edge to the satisfactory training programme that already existed. George had not left his job but the job had been adjusted to fit him. The result was that the company not only kept a highly effective trainer, but they developed a very motivated trainer who would continue to bring a degree of sharpness to their training programme – a key element in their fast-changing business.

Is your 'fit' good enough? What changes could you make to get the fit above the 70 per cent threshold?

Same job, different organization

The ability of a company to develop a job in order to develop the person in the job is a critical factor in keeping motivation high. But there are occasions when the nature of the company is such that the job simply cannot be developed. It is not necessarily a criticism to comment that a given job cannot always be developed for a particular individual. The reasons that underlie the decision not to develop a particular job may be varied and complex. The company may decide that the individual concerned is not someone that they wish to develop in the longer term because of factors unrelated to the particular skills of that individual.

Equally, an individual may decide that they do not fit the corporate culture well and would like to do the same job in an organization that is willing to develop the role over time. In this case the fit that is required is not only related to the job itself but has to do with finding a good fit between the values and personality of an individual and the culture of the organization that employs them.

Different job, same organization

Emily was in the unusual position of having to find a different job in the same organization in order to remain in the employ of the company! She had taken a role as executive assistant to the chief executive. The company saw the post as a two-year appointment, after which they tended to appoint someone new to the post. Emily had enjoyed the job, because she loved the variety and the feeling of being close to the place where decisions were made, and she liked to make a 'key' contribution to whatever task or team she was involved in. She had certainly been able to make a central contribution to the company and to her boss, not least because she had been able to anticipate the needs of her boss to an extraordinary extent.

As Emily contemplated a move, hopefully elsewhere in the company, she realized that the motivated abilities that had worked well in her role as executive assistant could serve her well elsewhere in the company. Her ability to foresee the needs of her boss was part of a strong planning element in her personal pattern. The particular company that she worked for had a need to engage in parliamentary lobbying as a crucial part of their business. Emily took her desire to make a key contribution and, together with her planning ability, developed a research role in the part of the company that coordinated relationships with Westminster. The outcome worked well for Emily and for her company.

How about you? Do you need to talk to someone about making a change?

Take a new direction

For significant numbers of people, especially in the second half of their lives, it simply is not possible to adjust the job or to find a related job elsewhere in the same organization. Often the problem has developed over time as a consequence of a promotional pattern that has not taken account of core motivations.

Chris was an engineer who just loved the sight, sound and smell of engines. His good analytical skills meant that he had been promoted a number of times. Given these skills, and his ability to create models and test them, the particular promotional route that he followed led him to a post in which he had to develop financial models for his company. He was good at his job, but it just didn't satisfy him. Money and finance are all very well, but they don't sound like engines and they don't smell like diesel! When Chris started to work through the 'Who Do You Think You Are?' process, he found that he had lots of work achievements in his early years and virtually none in the last 10 years – all his later achievements centred around the interest he had in 'classic cars' and all were outside his work. Chris, like so many others who have become detached from key motivational factors, had to make a decision as to whether or not he should make a radical change and take a new direction.

In past times many have solved the problem of growing dissatisfaction by taking early retirement. While leaving a demotivating job can certainly reduce pain and stress, it does not by itself lead to a satisfying change. Taking a totally different direction offers the possibility of constructing a working environment that takes full account of the abilities that motivate you. But that will only happen if you have a good awareness of what your abilities and motivations really are.

3. What have I learnt?

This is the moment to revisit the exercises that you conducted in Chapters 3–5. As you thought about your achievements, how did you summarize your key motivated abilities? What is it about the way you are that causes you to enjoy doing certain tasks again and again and again? Bearing in mind the lessons you have learnt from those earlier exercises, consider carefully the options you might have.

What did you learn from Exercise 11 (p. 131), where you were mapping your motivation with your current context? Do you feel that your job is basically satisfying, but it simply needs to be developed further in order to fit you better? If so, list the key changes that you would like to make in order to produce that better shape to your job. We are going to revisit this option below.

Alternatively, do you feel that the core problem is related more to the organization that you work for than to the role you have? Is this the moment to begin looking for a similar role within another organization? If you were to look for a post with another company, what would be the important factors or values that would mark the next organization as different from the one you are in now? Even if you were to look for another job which is broadly similar to the one that you enjoy doing now, are there any amendments that you would like to make in a potentially new situation?

Is the company that you work for now sufficiently large and/or flexible to work with you on constructing a different role within the same organization? Do you feel that those kinds of options are not really open to you? How could you be certain of your options one way or another? Who would you talk to within the organization to investigate your alternatives?

As you think about your life, in all that you have been learning about yourself as we have worked through the 'Who Do You Think You Are?' process, what's the 'balance' like for you? Please complete Exercise 12. Give this a good hour's thought.

Exercise 12

Adjusting the fine-tune balance

In the light of your new understanding of yourself through the 'Who Do You Think You Are?' process, use this exercise to help you address the problem of balance in your life. Please give some thought to the following scales. Each line represents a continuum of dimensions on which you either feel 'in balance' or 'out of balance'. Mark on the scale just where you are *now* (use an 'x') and then where you would like to be (use an 'o') in your next job/role. After each mark, add a brief description of what that *means to you*.

Example:

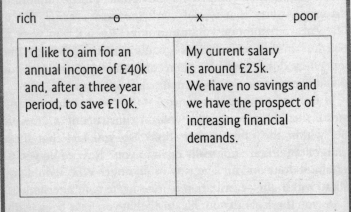

rich ——————— o ———— x ———— poor

I'd like to aim for an annual income of £40k and, after a three year period, to save £10k.	My current salary is around £25k. We have no savings and we have the prospect of increasing financial demands.

Please feel free to construct your own scales if these do not define everything for you.

Balance sheet

rich ——————————————————— poor

independent ——————————— dependent
on others

no risk ——————————————— risk

travelling ——————————————— no travel
a great deal

insecurity/
entrepreneurial ———————————————— security/
context   assured
                                 resource base

time spent
with others ————————————————— time spent
on a team   by myself

short project ————————————————— long project
duration   duration

project numbers ———————————————— project numbers
many/small   few/large

internal activity
(administer/manage/————————
build systems)

external activity
(clients/events/key
external resources)

4. What matches your motivation and how can you communicate this to others?

Remember the exercise we asked you to do at the end of Chapter 5 – writing your ideal job or role (Step 10, p. 107). We weren't thinking there of the world of rewards – a high salary, an unlimited expense account, a luxury company car and extensive travel with no accountability. Your ideal job description outlines what you would see yourself actually doing in a job. What actions did you feature? For example, did you describe yourself developing new ideas or things? Did you focus on how you love to work in support of others or with others in a team? Did you prefer a role that involves you researching, planning, writing, discovering, improving, teaching or demonstrating what you know to others? Take your ideal job statement and the description of yourself in the flow from Exercise 8 (p. 110). Since this is your 'stuff', this is (or at least should be) interesting to you. If you've done the work conscientiously, it should also be fairly rich in detail. However, there is far too much information for anyone else.

If you are to have any chance of securing for yourself a new role that matches your motivation, then you need two things. You need the 'matching' tool that we created in Chapter 6, where we developed the 'pig-in-mud scenario' and the 'scenario from hell' (Exercise 9, p. 123). This should give you the confidence to go out and start exploring, knowing that as you gather data about any possible option, you have something with which to compare what you find. You also need to be able to talk about yourself and communicate who you are in ways that don't put people off or bore them. That means more 'wordsmithing' with your material!

If you are going to communicate clearly to others at least some of what you have learnt from going through this process, then you need to know how to represent your material. At the moment there is too much detail. The best way to think about representing who you are is to think of a computer's 'interface' with the 'world'. The best computers all use a 'graphical interface' (long gone are the days of the dreaded DOS!). Graphical interfaces have the advantage of being simple – at least they appear simple to the user. That is to say, the user doesn't need to work hard to understand and get what's available – someone else has already thought very hard about how the information you need has been presented to you! Icons and scroll-bars present 'headline' information. If you want more information, it's there, it's available – all you have to do is 'ask'. Information is screened so that it's only available if the user wants it. The *Windows* concept is one of apparent simplicity based upon substantial in-depth knowledge. In presenting your strengths to others, you too need to have a *Windows* mentality.

So you need to convert the complex portrait that you have created for yourself (i.e. your description of your ideal job and of the 'flow' of your motivation) into something like the *Windows* menu bar. Exercise 13 is meant to help you to work on this:

Exercise 13

Learning how to communicate

1 Take the description of your ideal job/role from Step 10b (p. 116) and the flow diagram that you prepared in Exercise 8 (p. 110).
2 Take the answers to the question about the role you like to play and the meaning that 'achievement' has for you, and think of a phrase that sums it all up and that others could relate to (e.g. 'I'm an experienced *project manager* who enjoys setting up new enterprises'; 'I'm a *specialist* in communication'; 'I'm an *entrepreneurial doer*').

3 Next, picture what you do as having *three* phases – a beginning, a middle and an end. What is characteristic about each phase for you? (E.g. 'I research things thoroughly'; 'I can turn good ideas into practical results'; 'I create a really good-quality end-product.')

4 What benefits result from what you do? (E.g. 'We don't often make the wrong decisions'; 'The job gets done'; 'Teamwork produces results.')

5 Write two lines for each phase, starting with the benefit.

Now, using your sentences in the box above, we are going to help you create a game-plan to go and talk to someone who needs to know who you are (your boss, your colleagues, your partner, your bank manager). Think of the context in which you would like to talk to them. Should you request a formal one-to-one? Should you 'engineer' an informal chat with them after work? Should you set up a time when you know that they won't be distracted?

When you have thought of a context in which they might be receptive, think of the reactions that they might have to a conversation about you. What might be their worst fears for such a conversation? How can you allay those fears? How can you help them to see what is so clear to you? Imagine what they might want to get from you in such a conversation. What are their 'wants and fears' and what are yours?

Exercise 14

Wants and fears

This should take you 30 minutes.

If I were to set up a conversation with my boss/my partner about who I am, I believe these would be their 'wants and fears':

Wants	**Fears**

These are my 'wants and fears' for such a conversation:

Wants	**Fears**

This is how I intend to address the fears so that I can get what I want from the conversation:

Chris, the engineer whom we mentioned above, rediscovered his love of engines through the 'Who Do You Think You Are?' process. He realized that he loved the tactile element of practical, hands-on involvement. Early on in his career he had worked as a test engineer. His analytical skills were useful in the testing element of his job. His promotion had resulted in the use only of his analytical skills and had missed out the essential element of the tactile. For Chris, it was virtually impossible to go back to test engineering. That world had changed beyond recognition. He needed to find a new set of circumstances which would utilize both his need for tactile involvement and his love of analysis. He found it by becoming the technical expert in a business acquisitions team. He was hands-on, in the field, getting amongst the engineers in the workshop as well as assisting the technical analysis.

Our motivated abilities will fit a wide range of situations, provided that the situations can be moulded to fully deploy our motivational pattern.

5. Who can support me in the process?

The 'road' we need to travel, as Scott Peck has observed, is difficult. That does not mean that we should avoid it, but it does mean that we may need some support.

Before thinking about support in relation to career development, it is important to remember that discovering who you are in relation to your motivation is *not* a cure for every ill or problem you have encountered. Arthur and Jill had a severe problem in relating to each other in their marriage. Learning how to talk about themselves in a way that the other person could understand and recognize was a good first step. Learning how to listen to each other was the next. Recognizing that 'it wasn't personal' helped each of them to accept the other's behaviour as less malevolent. Uncovering their core motivations helped them to understand something else about each other, but it didn't address the core problem in their marriage. As Rebecca West (wife of the blatant philanderer H. G. Wells) observed: 'Understanding isn't forgiveness, it's just understanding!' Discovering who you think you are represents a way of taking forward your motivations in ways that will satisfy the healthy you. It will not fix the parts of you that may be damaged by severe trauma, or even deal with specific points of pain that have tended to emerge and re-emerge at different life stages. These issues require different means of support, and it is not our purpose in writing this book to address those specific questions.

Even apart from the need to find support for areas of damage, the issues of self-discovery outlined by the processes in this book are sufficiently complex to require further support. What is available?

Other sources of personal insight and wisdom

There are lots of self-insight tools available. Some of them can give you really useful information about yourself – psychometric testing, for example. For those who know the field well, there is a wide range of psychometric tests available. The best known and probably the most widely used is the Myers Briggs approach, originally developed by the US military. There are many others available. You should not be afraid to use other tests in addition to this book. They will all tell you something about yourself that can add to the total picture that you have of yourself. Other self-help books might be useful too.

People who know us well

Those who know us well can be really good sources of support and feedback. You may have close friends, colleagues or family members who can offer a valuable perspective. You might like to try out some of the conclusions that you have come to as a result of working with this book. Consult with those you trust. Ask them whether what you have discovered about yourself through this book matches with what they know of you. Can they offer some additional insight into the way in which your discoveries might be applied? If you don't get enough feedback from others, could you organize an informal 360° feedback process with them (i.e. a process of getting feedback from everyone around you – your boss, your peers and your subordinates)? Use the framework provided in Exercise 14 as the basis of your getting a perspective on how your gifts and motivations impact on others in your world.

The human resources / personnel department of your company/ organization

Many companies have a well developed human resources (personnel) department which you may be able to consult in terms of what you are discovering about yourself. A good department may be able to help you apply what you are learning in the work context, may support the exploration you have been doing, and may have access to other means of support.

The SIMA consultancy business and other consultancies or short courses

The approach we have outlined in this book is based upon a more comprehensive approach developed by People Management International. If you would like further help in either sorting through what you are learning about yourself or in how to apply it, you could always seek some professional input. Though the primary focus of our business is corporate, we do provide a career planning process for individuals based exclusively on the SIMA process and its modified form, the 'Who Do You Think You Are?' process. Naturally, as a business we will make a charge for this. We also have trained Associates who use both the SIMA process and the 'Who Do You Think You Are?' process. You can contact one of the addresses listed in the section 'What Next?' (p. 181) for details of our more advanced, more personal consultancy or our short courses.

Exercise 15

A 'perceptions' exercise

Copy and enlarge this box and give it to three or four
people whom know you well. Ask them to help you get a
view of your strengths and weaknesses. Make sure you ask
more than one person.

**Please complete this exercise and give it to ....
Feel free to use more space.**

*The following are my perceptions of you based upon my
experience of you.*

I see your strengths as …	I see your weaknesses as …
•	•
•	•
•	•
•	•
•	•
•	•
•	•
I find the following *helpful/ facilitative* to me personally in the way you work:	I find the following *frustrating* to me personally in the way you work:
•	•
•	•
•	•
•	•
•	•
•	•
•	•

6. Set personal goals

Turning what someone once called 'someday thoughts' into reality means setting personal goals that you mean to achieve. Before you arrive at a goal-setting process, it is often good to put down a marker of where you are now. One way of doing that is through the discipline of writing a journal. Essentially that means keeping a record or journal of your key thoughts and feelings: where do you think you are in your life's journey at this moment in time, and how do you feel about where you are? As events move on, you might take time, either every day or even just once a week, to record the major changes that you notice. Taking time to note your progress will surprise and encourage you along the way.

Goals are steps along the way to achieving a broader aim. Your broader aim in this context is to be in a 'life situation', including your job or major occupation, which is fulfilling. Assuming that you are not yet in that situation, it is worth setting some goals to help you towards that end.

A good goal tells you what you want to accomplish, by when, in a form that is measurable so that you will be able to know whether or not you have achieved it. For example, 'I will complete all the exercises in this book within the next 30 days.' In formulating such a goal you will know what you have to do and whether or not you have done it in the required time-frame. A poor goal would be something like, 'I want to feel better about my life.' That might be a desirable aim, but it is not an actionable goal.

Establish the steps or goals that you would need to complete in order to meet your broader aim. Your precise circumstances and preferences will determine both the broader aim and the goals that you would need to use to reach that end. So, for example, if your broader aim is taken as making a major reassessment of your job with a view to finding a more satisfying role, then your steps might be something like the following:

1   Complete the exercises in *Who Do You Think You Are?* within one month.
2   Check out your conclusions with five people who know you well by the end of the second month.
3   Work on a CV that really reflects the person you are. Turn what is merely a dead chronicle of past experiences into a dynamic marketing tool that really sells 'you at your best' by the end of the thirteenth week.
4   Test the CV out on your five chosen friends by the end of the fourteenth week.
5   Research suitable jobs within three months.
6   Assuming that you have adequate training/qualifications to begin applying for such jobs, apply for at least five appropriate posts within four months.
7   If you don't have the training, research where and how you might get that training.
8   Aim to have closed a contract on a new job within six months, or begin a review process to analyse why you have so far been unsuccessful, and set new goals in relation to that review.

Goals are supplemented by making plans to achieve your goals. Your particular situation may be such that the list above would not be the right steps to take or the right goals to set. But whatever your goals, you need to think through a plan of action that will cause your goals to be met. Simply setting the goals does not by itself enable the event to take place. Make sure that you have plans in place that relate to each of your goals. For example, if your goal is to research suitable jobs within three months, how are you going to do that? Is it best to talk to people in the industry, or to consult a specialist recruitment company, or to scrutinize trade journals and newspapers, or to write to leading companies, or something else? You need a plan to allow the goal to be reached.

Please complete Exercise 16 overleaf, a simple action-planning tool that asks you to commit yourself to some specific actions (e.g. as shown to you by Exercise 13, p. 151). It then asks you to consider the impact on others that may result from what you are thinking of doing.

7. Seize tomorrow

The question of what people believe at a deep level about life is an important hidden factor in the way we act. For example, do you believe that fundamentally life is malevolent – that one way or another, in a way that is hard to explain, the basic truth about life is that life itself is out to get you? So no matter what you do, you cannot really expect anything good to happen.

Or do you believe the exact opposite? Do you think that, despite some setbacks, basically life is benevolent – that, even if you make mistakes, there is good waiting to be found; that joy, happiness, beauty, goodness and contentment are available in worthwhile measure, and are not just the special preserve of the very few?

In all probability you will believe both of these things at different times of your life. The more that we are operating in a set of circumstances which really damage our creative abilities, the more likely it is that we will tend towards the view that life is an extremely depressing kind of experience. It is fairly obvious that the more successful we are in finding a situation which fits us like a glove, the more we will feel positive in our evaluation of the way life is.

The likelihood is that you are not yet in that best-fit situation, and the problem is that making a move towards that situation requires an energy level that flows more easily from us when we are in circumstances that draw out the best in us. Our ability to make the transition or to seize the future when all is not well is an important element in our future success.

Exercise 16

Action planning

This should take you 30 minutes.

What do you intend to do/achieve as a result of reaching this point in the book?	Achieved by?
1.	
2.	
3.	
4.	
5.	

When you have completed this list, choose one of the proposals and examine its implications by using the following diagram:

	For myself	**Involving others**
Benefits or pay-offs		
Downsides or sacrifices		

How can you minimize the 'pain' for yourself in this process?

How can you minimize the 'pain' for others in this process?

What makes the difference? Some seem to have the ability to overcome adversity as if difficulty was simply a welcome challenge. We are not all 'wired' like that. Some need encouragement along the way. The hope of both the authors of this book is that the contents of these pages will contain those moments of encouragement that will help you to seize tomorrow.

We started this book with a story about a friend of ours who visited a world where people were expected to knuckle under, fit in and accept whatever role/job they were given. As we have worked with you through this book we have tried to encourage you to understand who you are, to celebrate the uniqueness you have, and to find ways of using that uniqueness so that you can find roles/jobs that better match who you are. We want you (as we quoted from Charles Handy earlier) to stand behind your own name-tag and to find pleasure and productivity in being who you are. We believe there's an ultimate truth here – a truth that Handy again identifies. He cites the story of the rabbi Zosya:

> There was a rabbi once, called Zuzya of Hannipol. He spent his life lamenting his lack of talent and his failure to be another Moses. One day God comforted him. 'In the coming world,' he said, 'we will not ask you why you were not Moses, but why you were not Zuzya.'

This is Me at My Best

Working Document

What do I think gets me started?

Evidence for this: words and phrases I have used that indicate *how* I get started.

What do I think keeps me going?

Evidence for this: words and phrases I have used that indicate *what* kept me going.

What do I do when I am motivated?

These seem to me to be ordered like this ...

Evidence for this: words and phrases I have used that indicate *what* I do when I am motivated.

This is what I like working with:
Intangibles

Tangibles

Data

People

Senses

Mechanisms (i.e. means I use)

What results and recognition do I seek?

Evidence for this: words and phrases I have used that indicate *what* results or recognition I seek.

What supports me to achieve?

Evidence for this: words and phrases I have used that indicate *what* supports me to achieve.

What role/roles do I seem to take in my achievements?

Evidence for this: words and phrases I have used that indicate *what* role I seem to take on in my achievements.

I find satisfaction in ...

Evidence for this: words and phrases I have used that indicate *what* I find satisfaction in.

This gets me started...

This keeps me going...

This supports me...

These are the results I seek...

Motivated Abilities I consistently use

What interests me?

Relationships/Roles I perform well in

Motivational Drives

This is Me at My Best

Sample form completed

What do I think gets me started?
New things, different things.
Problems to solve, things that aren't working.

Evidence for this: words and phrases I have used that indicate *how* I get started.

'It was the first time I had done it.'
'I had never been there before.'
'It was stuck so I had to do something.'
'He said to me, "So what are you going to do with it?"'
'My first bike.'
'My first car.'
'We'd never encountered something like this.'

'It was new to me.'
'Well, I thought, at least it's different.'
'I was interested because I hadn't worked on one before.'
'No one else could sort it, so I had to.'
'Going round the scrap yards I found some things I could adapt.'

What do I think keeps me going?

Application involved, useful outcomes, possible difficulties to overcome.
The potential involved, the possibilities.
Hidden resources that need to be uncovered.

Evidence for this: words and phrases I have used that indicate *what* kept me going.

'I stuck at it.'
'Nothing was going to stop me.'
'I wouldn't give up.'
I had to make this thing work.'
'"What do I do with it?", I said.'
'I kept on thinking, tomorrow I will be able to drive this.'
'We saw the value we could get from it.'
'No one else saw the possibilities.'
'I like reading manuals because they help you do things.'
'She didn't have much self-worth but I thought she could do it.'
'My friends all thought I was crazy.'
'Every night without fail I was there working at it.'
'I kept saying to the team, "What's the point of this?"'
'It worked and I could apply it.'
'Even in the rain it was hard.'
'The water was very cold so it put everyone off.'

What do I do when I am motivated?
Reading, studying
analysing, dissecting
organizing, sorting,
planning, experimenting
writing
initiating
putting things together, building
picturing, designing
changing, adapting, extending

These seem to me to be ordered like this …
1) reading and studying and understanding
2) analysing and experimenting, playing with
3) picturing, designing, organizing, sorting
4) building, assembling, changing, adapting
5) communicating, initiating, waiting

Evidence for this: words and phrases I have used that indicate *what* I do when I am motivated.

'Read about it.'
'I studied very hard.'
'I had to analyse the problem.'
'The numbers didn't add up.'
'The whole thing was worth a lot now.'
'I had to adapt what I had.'
'I saw I could take it a stage further.'
'I sorted everything into piles.'
'We built it together.'
'We experimented.'
'We planned the whole thing.'
'I put it together well.'
'I judged this was the wrong way.'

'I designed.'
'I explained to him.'
'So, I wrote a paper.'
'I pictured what it would look like.'
'I like to know what standard I have to reach.'
'Basically, it was my idea I sold him.'
'I put my thoughts down on paper.'

This is what I like working with:

Intangibles	concepts, pictures in my mind, ideas for things
Tangibles	machinery, cars, bikes, gadgets
Data	details, logistics
People	individuals
Senses	physically touching things, handling tangible things
Mechanisms (i.e. means I use)	models, methods, techniques, tips of the trade, becoming an expert, technology

What results and recognition do I seek?

Effectiveness, the thing working well.
Meeting the challenge set.
A finished product, a tangible outcome.
Status, respect, being valued by others.

Evidence for this: words and phrases I have used that indicate *what* results or recognition I seek.

'I impressed my friends with it.'
'It worked.'
'I could then use it to play games.'

'No one else in the street had one.'
'I liked being able to mix with "big wigs".'
'My name was on the door.'
'You could pick it up and touch it.'
'We stood back and admired what we had made.'
'As a result of this, I was invited to join the club.'
'All the girls in the class thought my picture was best.'
'I was in a class of my own when it came to art.'
'It was good to get it done.'
'My report was published and was well reviewed.'
'We won the award.'
'I proved to myself I could do it.'
'I got promoted to the next level.'
'You could see the quality of what we'd made.'

What supports me to achieve?

I need preparation time, time to get everything ready and I like some initial support from someone I respect and trust.

Evidence for this: words and phrases I have used that indicate *what* supports me to achieve.

'I talked it through with my boss.'
'I knew he was there even though I was on my own.'
'He and I discussed it first.'
'I respected him so I listened to him.'
'There was always someone on the end of the phone.'
'I had the time I needed to get the study done.'
'I liked being able to pore over the books.'

What role/roles do I seem to take in my achievements?

As a solo performer.
As a contributor.
As an individual with my own distinctive task and role.

Evidence for this: words and phrases I have used that indicate *what* role I seem to take on in my achievements.

'I did it completely.'
'This was all my own work.'
'I was the top scorer in the match.'
'I took the training from start to finish.'
'There were others involved but this was my contribution.'
'I showed myself how to do it.'
'I know what was expected of me so I just got on with it.'
'I was on the time – no one else.'
'It was all mine.'
'I became the world's expert on this.'

I find satisfaction in ...

Zone 4: effect I can have on the 'object'.
Making things work, fixing things.
Zone 5: power zone. Comprehending them so they can be fixed.

Evidence for this: words and phrases I have used that indicate *what* I find satisfaction in.

'I mastered the subject completely.'
'It was broken, now it's fixed.'

'Nobody knew more than me on this.'
'I concentrate on the technical knowledge I need to do the job.'
'I am still trying to master the whole thing.'
'Correcting the errors until it worked.'
'Getting it to fly smoothly.'
'I did it one year and was invited back the next.'
'We had solved the problem.'
'I ended up with a brand new ash frame, an exact copy of the original.'
'It worked.'
'People didn't think I could do it, but I did.'
'It's good to sit on the patio and think, I did all that.'
'We could see that the thing was effective.'
'My approach was vindicated.'
'It did what it was supposed to do.'

This gets me started...

New things, different things.
Problems to solve, things that aren't working.

This keeps me going...

Application involved, useful outcomes, possible difficulties to overcome.
The potential involved, the possibilities.
Hidden resources that need to be uncovered.

This supports me...

I need preparation time, time to get everything ready, and I like some initial support from someone I respect and trust.

These are the results I seek...

Effectiveness, the thing working well.
Meeting the challenge set.
A finished product, a tangible outcome.
Status, respect, being valued by others.

Motivated Abilities I consistently use

1) reading and studying and understanding
2) analysing and experimenting, playing with
3) picturing, designing, organizing, sorting
4) building, assembling, changing, adapting
5) communicating, initiating, writing

What interests me?

Concepts, pictures in my mind, ideas for things.
Machinery, cars, bikes, gadgets.
Details, logistics.
Individuals.
Physically touching things, handling tangible things.
Models, methods, techniques, tips of the trade, becoming an expert, technology.

Relationships/Roles I perform well in

As a solo performer.
As a contributor.
As an individual with my own distinctive task and role.

Motivational Drives

Zone 4: effect I can have on the 'object'.
Making things work, fixing things.
Zone 5: power zone. Comprehending them so they can be fixed.

What Next?

The 'Who Do You Think You Are?' process has been developed by SIMA (UK) Ltd, a management consultancy that specializes in helping people, as individuals and in organizations, to make better use of their strengths. The process outlined here is based upon the System for Identifying Motivated Abilities (SIMA), the distinctive assessment process of SIMA (UK) Ltd. SIMA (UK) Ltd is the United Kingdom licence holder for the process from People Management International (PMI). PMI has over 35 years of experience in using and applying SIMA to problems of motivation and organizational effectiveness.

Further professional career help based upon the 'Who Do You Think You Are?' process is available. This service is a series of *four* meetings during which we work with you to work out your motivational pattern, help you to see the career implications of it, then work with you to apply what you've learnt to your life. If you would like to know more about this service, please keep all the work you've done here and give us a call. We will provide you with the name of a trained professional to work with you. We also provide consultancy services to organizations based upon the full SIMA process. Finally, we do provide training to suitable consultants who are interested in using either the 'Who Do You Think You Are?' process or the SIMA process.

For further details of any of these services and current costs contact:

SIMA (UK) Ltd,
Clockhouse Barn,
Sugworth Lane,
Radley,
Oxford,
OX14 2HX,
United Kingdom
Tel: 01865 321123
Fax: 01865 326611
Email: simauk@patrol.i-way.co.uk
Or visit our website: www.sima.co.uk

For consultants outside the UK interested in becoming part of the People Management International group of companies, please contact:

People Management International LLC,
1 Darling Drive,
Avon,
Connecticut,
CT 06001,
United States
Tel: 001 860 678 8900
Fax: 001 860 676 1130
Email: kvarriale@jobfit-pmi.com
Or visit their website: www.jobfit-pmi.com

Notes

Chapter 1

1 For a detailed discussion of the relationship between stress at work and health factors see Cary L. Cooper, Rachel D. Cooper and Lynn H. Eaker, *Living with Stress* (Penguin, 1988), pp. 80ff.

2 Jeff Davidson, *The Complete Idiot's Guide to Managing Stress* (Alpha Books, 1997), p. 12.

3 Charles Handy, *The Age of Unreason* (Century Hutchinson, 1989), p. 203.

Chapter 2

1 If you run your own consultancy and would be interested in being trained in the full SIMA process and joining the People Management International network, please contact Ms Kathleen Variale on 001 860 678 8900, or try the People Management International website on www.jobfit-pmi.com

2 Adapted from Rosemary Boam and Paul Sparrow, *Designing and Achieving Competency: A competency based approach to developing people and organisations* (McGraw-Hill, 1992), p. 17.

Chapter 4

1 The quotation comes from a Gestalt thinker called Smuts. It is cited in an excellent introduction to the work of Fritz Perls: Retruska Clarkson and Jennifer MacKewn, *Fritz Perls* (Sage, 1993), p. 54. Other work by Clarkson and

MacKewn is equally helpful in understanding the complexities of Gestalt: see Retruska Clarkson, *Gestalt Counselling in Action* (Sage, 1989); Jennifer MacKewn, *Developing Gestalt Counselling* (Sage, 1997).

2. For a fuller description of the 'Gestalt Cycle of Awareness', please refer to a series of articles in *The Training Officer* by Susan Clayton and Trevor Bentley: 'Gestalt – a philosophy of change', Part 1, Jan./Feb. 1996, Vol. 32, No. 1, pp. 5–7; Part 2, Mar. 1996, Vol. 32, No. 2, pp. 48–9; Part 3, Apr. 1996, Vol. 32, No. 3, pp. 72–4; Part 4, May 1996, Vol. 32, No. 4, pp. 106–7; Part 5, Jun. 1996, Vol. 32, No. 5, pp. 149–51; Part 6, Jul./Aug. 1996, Vol. 32, No. 6, pp. 180–81.

Sue and Trevor also run a training programme in Gestalt entitled 'Gestalt in organisations'. For further details, contact: Gestalt in Organisations, Upper Steanbridge Mill, Slad, Stroud, Gloucestershire GL6 7QE. Tel: 01452 813908. Fax: 01452 814071. Email: Parsifalwiz@ compuserve.com